PRINCE CHARLES

AND THE ARCHITECTURAL DEBATE

WREN'S MONUMENT OBSCURED, PHOTO SELECTED BY HRH THE PRINCE OF WALES
FROM THE EXHIBITION AT THE V&A

PHOTO SELECTED BY HRH THE PRINCE OF WALES, FROM THE EXHIBITION AT THE V&A

An Architectural Design Profile

PRINCE CHARLES
AND THE ARCHITECTURAL DEBATE

ADSHEAD & RAMSEY, AMMONITE ORDER, DUCHY OF CORNWALL ESTATE, PHOTO COURTESY JOHN MELVIN

ACADEMY EDITIONS · LONDON / ST. MARTIN'S PRESS · NEW YORK

Acknowledgements

This issue of *Architectural Design* coincides with the publication of HRH The Prince of Wales's book *A Vision of Britain: A Personal View of Architecture* published by Doubleday and the opening of an exhibition with the same title at London's Victoria and Albert Museum, a series of media events including a major television programme and the re-showing of 'The Visions of Britain', a well-known programme produced by Christopher Martin who contributes here the opening essay. We are grateful to the many architects who have contributed material to this publication and especially to Leon Krier for material relating to his Master Plan for Poundbury near Dorchester, to John Thompson and the organisers of the Poundbury Planning Weekend. We thank the following for their help in the preparation of this issue: the Director and Trustees of the Tate Gallery for permission to reproduce part of the Proceedings of the Academy Forum at the Tate on 'Prince Charles and the Architects'; the contributors to this issue, especially to Christopher Martin, Charles Knevitt and Michael Collins who responded so positively at such short notice; John Melvin, for supplying a number of his own photos and for his help in connection with the article *Classicism in British Architecture*; Maureen Read at the Times/RIBA Community Enterprise Scheme 1988-89 for help and material in connection with the Community Architecture projects; Simon Jenkins and Richard Rogers for allowing us to reprint here their articles; and Steven Brooke Studios, Florida for supplying us with their excellent photos from Seaside, Florida.

Front Cover: Leon Krier, Plan of the first Middle Farm quarter, 1989, photo courtesy the architect; *Back Cover*: Wren's Monument Obscured, photo from *A Vision of Britain*; *Inside Front Cover*: Demetri Porphyrios, House in Chepstow Villas, 1988, photo courtesy the architect; *Inside Back Cover*: Leon Krier, Belvedere, Seaside, Florida, 1988, photo by Steven Brooke Studios, Florida; *Half-Title & Frontis*: photos from *A Vision of Britain*; *Title Page*: photo John Melvin; *Contents Page*: The Times/RIBA Community Enterprise Awards Scheme: Ashcott Village Hall, Bridgwater, photo by Bill Warhurst.

Christopher Martin
pp 6-15: pp 6, 7, 12, 15, photos from *A Vision of Britain*; p 8, photo by Steve Bellasco; p 10, photos John Thompson.

Academy Forum at the Tate
pp 16-23: p 16, photo from *A Vision of Britain*; all illustrations supplied by the authors.
Ethics and Prince Charles
pp 24-29: Illustration on page 30 courtesy James Stirling, Michael Wilford & Associates; p 35, photo from *A Vision of Britain*.
Charles Knevitt
pp 36-39: p 36, photo by Steve Bellasco; p 39, photo by Martin Charles, supplied by the author.
Hunt Thompson
pp 40-43: All material supplied by the architects.
Community Architecture
pp 44-45: All material supplied by the Times/RIBA Community Enterprise Scheme.
Leon Krier: Master Plan for Poundbury Development in Dorchester
pp 46-55: All material supplied by the architect.
Classicism in British Architecture
pp 56-63: all material supplied by the architects; p 56, photo by Steven Brooke Studios, Florida; p 58 & p 61 below, paintings by Carl Laubin; p 59 above & p 62, photos John Melvin, p 62, photo El Wakil.
Max Hutchinson
pp 64-65: photo and extracts the RIBA.
Richard Rogers
pp 66-69: reproduced by kind permission of the author; p 66, illustration Royal Academy of Arts.
Simon Jenkins
p 70: reproduced by kind permission of the author.
New Town Ordinances & Codes
pp 71-75: p 71, photo by Steven Brooke Studios, Florida; codes and ordinances provided by the architects.
Demetri Porphyrios
pp 76-81: all material supplied by the architect.
Florentine New Towns
pp 82-88: extract and illustrations reproduced by kind permission of David Friedman from *Florentine New Towns: Urban Design in the Middle Ages*, an Architectural History Foundation book published by the MIT Press, Cambridge, MA at £40.50.

Editor: Dr Andreas C Papadakis

First published in Great Britain in 1989 by *Architectural Design*
an imprint of the
ACADEMY GROUP LTD, 7 HOLLAND STREET, LONDON W8 4NA
ISBN: 1-85490-021-8 (UK)

The Publishers and Editor do not hold themselves
responsible for the opinions expressed by the writers
of articles or letters in this magazine
Copyright of articles and illustrations
may belong to individual writers or artists
Architectural Design Profile 79 is published as part of *Architectural Design* Vol 59 5/6-1989
Published in the United States of America by
ST MARTIN'S PRESS, 175 FIFTH AVENUE, NEW YORK 10010
ISBN: 0-312-04048-2 (USA)

Printed and bound in Singapore

Contents

ASHCOTT VILLAGE HALL, BRIDGWATER, SEE PAGE 44

When Canaletto painted the view from Somerset House in the 18th century, the City of London rivalled Venice, another city built upon the tide, and was no less fair.

Much has happened to the view that Canaletto painted. A scheme to put another tower block between the Nat West Tower and St Paul's was only narrowly defeated this year.

CHRISTOPHER MARTIN
'Second Chance'

London, the biggest building site in Europe. A spectacular look towards Westminster Abbey with the Old Bailey on the left and the spire of Wren's St Bride's in Fleet Street still holding its own on the right.

Christopher Martin has been producing films on architecture for a number of years and, with *A Vision of Britain*, has fulfilled a significant role in focusing public attention on the controversies of the architectural debate, emerging as an influential critic in his own right. Here he discusses the consequences of the Prince's interventions and the problems confronting developers, attempting to find a consensus amid the conflicting visions of the 80s.

The phrase 'second chance' was used by the Prince of Wales in his famous Mansion House Speech in December 1987 and in his BBC TV film *A Vision of Britain*. 'We have this second chance. Pray God', he said, 'we can get it right this time'. The 'first chance' when we famously got it wrong was in the great post-war rebuilding of Britain. Few of even his fiercest critics disagree with the Prince's indictment of historic city centres devastated by planners ('worse that the Luftwafe'); utopian social experiments that led to the tower block and the eradication of old communities, the destruction of local identity, and the defacement of not just the cities and towns but the countryside of Britain which had once been 'a wonder of the world'.

Fewer within the architectural profession agreed with his prescriptions for the future. After a pause to draw breath following the Prince's assault, some architects have begun to counter-attack, enjoying the media possibilities of a situation where if 'Prince Slams Architects' gets the headlines, so too can 'Architects Slam Prince'. The slamming can be seen as an enjoyable way of stimulating what has become known as the 'debate' on Britain's architecture and environment. With the *A Vision of Britain* exhibition opening at the V&A and the Prince's book coming out simultaneously, the debate shows little sign of going quiet. It seems entirely in tune with the adversarial way in which matters are conducted in this country – in the courts and in parliament.

It is not necessarily the best way of working out exactly how this country is going to take the 'second chance'; with what styles, with what materials, with what technology, with what sensitivity to the changing needs of society. Rather it has fixed in people's minds extreme positions – as if there was nothing between the opinions of and the buildings designed by Richard Rogers and Quinlan Terry. But is it possible that between the two extremes some kind of consensus can be found, upon which some sort of shared ideas of excellence might be formed and from which planning and design can shake off its sense of furious introspection? Is there, within the evolving forms of modern architecture, a hitherto hidden human face which will endear it to a broad public?

The Prince can claim to have made his point and refers to the thousands of letters of support he received after the film went out last October – and he still gets a huge batch every month from people who turn to him as a somewhat unlikely, but very effective, 'voice' of the common man in a world dominated by contemptuous professionals.

The Prince is seen by his supporters as the voice of sanity; expressing what few in high places have ever expressed before, that something is terribly wrong with a country's culture when it is inexplicable to the vast majority of its citizens. Not just architecture but music that has no tune or melody, painting (where such exists) that bears no resemblance to any perceived 'reality', poetry that is unfathomable, and sculpture that is as baffling as the painting but inflicted increasingly on public places. There its sharp and uncompromising or alternatively whimsical and 'witty' presence fills the passer-by, who suspects (with some justice) that somewhere along the line he has paid for it, with resentment and anger against the 'progressive' people

*Man of Destiny? Architect Leon Krier prepares to meet the people of Dorchester at an ambitious 'participation' exercise,
mounted to find out what the community wanted from the most 'ambitious exercise in urban design this century'.*

who seem to like all these things and have embedded themselves in the cultural institutions of the country strongly enough to impose their liberal, forward-looking, tastes on everyone else.

On the other hand Rogers is seen to be as about as progressive as you can get and therefore he is a cherished totem of the Modernist cause. He is a glamorous and on his day articulate spokesman for the forces of democracy, progress and the need for what he calls a 'new ethic' – the exact nature of which has yet to be revealed but which, once adopted, promises to bring about the long-delayed conversion of the populace to an enthusiasm for the rich possibilities of modern life and modern art so that they will like not just the Lloyd's building, which as Rogers says is already terrifically popular with visitors, but by extension Gilbert and George, Andy Warhol, 'new' music and painting.

If the cultural divide does represent a sort of 'left' and 'right', does the middle-ground have any more chance of success than its political counterpart has had?

The debate rages at a vital time. The 'second chance' has come at a time when what is being built, not just in London – the docks, the City, King's Cross – but all over Britain, in Birmingham, Cardiff, Glasgow, Newcastle, Leeds and Liverpool, will transform the look and character of the country in the next decade. The scale of the changes will in many cases exceed what was done in the 50s and 60s. The building boom caters for our supposed need for new sorts of buildings and complexes of buildings, shaped by the new demands and advanced technologies of post-industrial Britain – heavily dependent on service industries, attuned to the new possibilities of 'leisure', and responsive to the limitless passion we are said to have for shopping. And beyond this is the demand for new housing – not just new estates but new villages and new towns in the heart of what would once have been regarded as inviolable countryside.

The repeat of the BBC film, the publication of the book, and a major museum exhibition ('. . . promising to be the most talked about exhibition of 1989' says the V&A modestly) will ensure that the Prince's views won't be forgotten and that his critics can no longer accuse him of not putting his theories into practice. Lately he has turned to exploring ways in which the environmental consequences of change *can* be made popular, an improvement of what was there before, even beautiful. The Duchy of Cornwall owns vast tracts of land in the west of England and dwindling but still appreciable chunks of London's Kennington. As Duke of Cornwall the Prince has a persuasive voice in shaping Duchy policy. Recently the Duchy, no longer content to exercise its stewardship in the traditional way, has become more involved in the design of new buildings, working with architects like John Simpson who see eye to eye with the Prince; becoming, in a word, more like developers. As the Prince has often said, 'I'm not against development.'

Just outside Dorchester are acres of Duchy land encircled by a new ring road which the council wants to develop to provide housing and other opportunities for their picturesque but somewhat stagnant county town. The council approached the Duchy and asked for proposals. Here was an opportunity for the Prince to put into practise the ideas he had declared in *A Vision of Britain*, a chance to build something that 'added to, rather than detracted from the English countryside'. This should not be another corner of England given over to charmless sprawl with the superstore as its principal focus. But the Duchy cannot be the instrument of experimental caprice – it has an obligation to be profitable. And the new development at Dorchester cannot just be a monument to enlightened Royal patronage. It hopes to be an example that other developers will follow and that will have a transforming effect on building everywhere. Leon Krier got the job of drawing up a master plan as a first stage in making the vision a reality. The choice of Krier disconcerted the Prince's

critics who are obliged to acknowledge Krier's reputation as a serious and brilliant theorist. He is not a man, however, who looks as if the Dorset vernacular has been uppermost in his thoughts over all the years of theorising and drawing that preceded the appointment. The tradition of which he is so zealous an advocate springs from the ancient world rather than that of Tess of the D'Urbervilles.

The impression you get from his first drawings and from an early model is indeed one of the forum and the baths rather than Thomas Hardy's Dorset. However, as he points out, the Renaissance came to Dorset too. Look at Blandford Forum, rebuilt after its own Great Fire in 1731 on good Classical lines. Krier sees no incongruity between the two traditions anyway. 'More important', he said to a recent meeting of the Art and Architecture Group in London, 'is that people want beauty around them. And everywhere they are denied it.' Instead they are given the neurotic expression of artists and architects who celebrate, if that's the right word, the tensions and anxieties of their age. 'People may need these things sometimes', he added doubtfully, 'but they also want harmony, reassurance, familiarity and beauty.' But such things in Dorchester have to be balanced against the needs of first time buyers, the requirements of car-parking, zoning or the absence of it, the benefits or otherwise of cul-de-sacs, shopping and the need for workshops and office space. Moreover the vision has to be squared with another strong element in the Prince's argument with the architectural establishment: Community Architecture.

True, there is no community to speak of actually living at Poundbury where the new town is to stand. But the wider community would certainly be consulted, and the voice of the people, so disastrously shut out from an actual say in the shaping of their own environment elsewhere, would certainly be heard in Dorchester.

Hunt Thompson Associates who are community architects with a reputation for almost evangelical zeal for their cause have already done work for the Duchy in Kennington and John Thompson was brought in to handle the consultation process. Very little was spared to ensure that the community was, indeed, not only consulted but seen to be consulted. Thompson organised what he calls a 'charette', an event which took place over five days in which experts from all over the country well versed in the intricacies of participation, fluent in such subjects as infrastructure and 'outreach', would help the people of Dorchester comprehend the destiny that beckoned them. And if they didn't like what was proposed, Thompson would be there to help articulate and make clear their objections. And at the 'charette', people would get to meet Leon Krier. Krier's encounter with the grass roots was awaited with some expectancy, as was the first public glimpse of what not only supporters but also critics were saying might be the most important exercise in urban design in Britain since the war – perhaps this century.

He was a howling success. White suited, white hatted, with a white silk scarf wound casually round the neck and wearing curiously designed dark glasses that made him look more like a figure from German Expressionist cinema than Gabriel Oak, Krier's very difference from what might have been expected was reassuring.

Here, clearly, was no smooth PR man selling a scheme by seductive manner and soft words. Krier on the contrary was forthright to the point of bluntness. If they, the 'community', didn't like what he was up to he'd go home and they could have the usual stuff. He acknowledged the difficulties, he admitted his ignorance about such matters as water ('Would the river Piddle be dried up by so many new demands on it?'), he thought cars parked in the road were a good thing (they cut down speed and are a buffer against noise), he thought business and work should

'I think it would look better over there . . .' An expert assessment of the prospect for Dorchester, viewed under the shadow of Maiden Castle.

A long hot summer's day at Poundbury Farm.

be muddled up with houses, and he thought the whole thing could be profitable if a long term view was taken rather than the instant maximisation of profits.

The people of Dorchester who attended, sheltered from the heat-wave in a large marquee tent or sweltering in a metal-roofed grain shed (necessary because it was dark and therefore the only place where slides could be shown) seemed well disposed to the scheme. They endured the experts, they submitted to the workshops. If the model had many puzzling features – what was that big, rotunda-like building actually *for*? – it certainly didn't look at all like a conventional housing estate. On the whole, I suspect, many of them wish the place could be left to the cows – just as it is. But given the inevitability of change, Krier's scheme seemed undoubtedly intriguing, and even HRH himself had come down to talk about it all with them. So John Thompson could claim that indeed the 'vision' was up and running and had the breath of popular approval behind it.

Meanwhile in another part of the country a huge new development of quite a different kind was about to hold *its* open day. But here champagne and salmon would be served rather than the tea and sandwiches of Poundbury Farm.

Stockley Park is a long way from the ancient turf of Dorsetshire; until recently the site was a vast rubbish dump, a mile or so north from Heathrow airport and handy for the M4. It is here that developer Stuart Lipton is building his vision, not for English yeomen, but a business park designed to attract the personnel of multi-national corporations. It is a colossal enterprise.

Lipton is providing lakes, public art, squash courts, a club and swimming pool. There will also be a golf-course. Famous modern architects like Norman Foster have been commissioned. The work is conforming to a master plan that has been drawn up by Sir Philip Dowson of Arup Associates. Sir Philip and Stuart Lipton are no strangers: Arups designed the first stages of Broadgate – the office mega-structure at London's Liverpool Street 'inaugurated' in a non-committal sort of way by the Prince. Arups won the competition Lipton organised to design the master plan for Paternoster Square – a scheme about which the Prince was anything but non-commital. Stockley Park has also been blessed by a Princely visit.

Stockley Park has a patron in Lipton with a reputation for being one of the country's most enlightened developers. Here, if anywhere perhaps, the brave new face of modern British architecture will be revealed. Nearly a thousand visitors – developers, architects, journalists and businessmen – turned up for the open day. The Foster-designed building is not a small one but they filled large parts of it. Not only was there modern architecture aplenty on show but ambitious landscaping as well. The largest living trees ever transplanted (from Belgium) were surviving the drought and helicopters were on hand to give aerial views of the complex, threaded together by a great avenue, lovingly incorporated into the master plan by Sir Philip. Nicholas Ridley had been billed to speak but, to Lipton's expressed irritation, he failed to come.

Lipton took me and a BBC film crew up in the helicopter. His pride in Stockley Park is evident – this is far more important and personal to him than anything else he has done – including Broadgate. He acknowledges a wry similarity between this scheme and Dorchester. But Stockley Park looks forward, it is in the idiom of its day, not yesterday. The Prince, Lipton says, must learn to look forward too. The elegantly shining, meticulously laid-out buildings, strangely white amid the green of the park, like Dorchester will be the tangible expression of a vision. Much is expected of Lipton.

It is increasingly said that the failures of modern architecture are as much to do with failures of patronage as the shortcomings of architects and planners. But developers have to show a return on capital quickly to satisfy all the pension fund investors and others who have put their millions at their disposal. The consequence has been the 'bottom line' architecture which makes up the vast majority of new development all over Britain. It is this endless proliferation of mediocre, ill-built and ugly development that should be – it is said – the target of the Prince; not the few examples we have in this country of outstanding work by architects like Stirling, Lasdun, Dowson, St John Wilson, who are utterly committed to the art of which they are masters and who moreover, if from a different position, share HRH's concern, even anguish, about the deteriorating environment.

Lipton is aware of his power, aware of the eyes watching whatever he touches, conscious of the responsibilities that his not unenviable position gives him. I found him surprisingly, if engagingly, candid about the difficulties he faces in making decisions which will effect where and how we live so formidably. How do you choose an architect, a style, in a country in which there is no consensus about what is 'good' or 'bad' architecture? Lipton sees himself as a patron of all good modern architecture. He would have worked with Quinlan Terry on Spitalfields had the cards fallen a different way. He's working with Rogers and Foster now.

Lipton confesses himself genuinely perplexed as to where to turn for advice. His attempts to bring the Prince on board at Paternoster Square, Broadgate and Stockley Park were not merely due to the obvious prestige the Royal association could give to the projects, but were also an attempt to connect with someone who had such clear and definite opinions and who seems to have no doubts at all about what is good and beautiful. Perhaps by now Lipton feels the Prince's views are, for the moment, too inflexible to be quite the source of inspiration he had hoped for, but there's no doubting his admiration for the Prince's certainty of mind.

Lipton doesn't claim to be the only developer with ambitions to add something of aesthetic as well as financial value to London. Andrew Wadsworth toils in the same vineyard, so to speak, and shares Lipton's concerns about the quality of buildings created by the current boom. Wadsworth seems less seduced by the stern canons of Modernism than Lipton; he and the architects he employs seem to inject a more personal note into their projects like New Concordia Wharf and Jacobs Island. Some people find it all a bit quirkey and undignified; it certainly seems a long way away from the august 'master planning' of Broadgate and Paternoster Square. But it's not just a question of scale; Wadsworth, one feels, is much less impressed by questions of modern architecture's ideological mission, and much more prepared to give enjoyable expression to his own tastes.

So where *do* developers like Lipton go for reassurance and advice when they propose to transform yet further acres of the capital? Their operations are hedged about by a thicket of planning regulations which to Lipton are the cause not of a better environment ('just look around you at Planner's London . . .') but of endless delays, compromises and huge expenses, merely adding to the general paralysis that prevents such economic vitality as we have being reflected in our architecture.

The Royal Fine Art Commission is one body to which Lipton turns hopefully and of which indeed he is – controversially – a member. To accusations that practising poachers shouldn't become gamekeepers, yet alone sit on the bench, the RFAC can claim that it badly needs the sheer knowledge that a successful large-scale developer can bring to their deliberations. Nevertheless they managed without one before and performed satisfactorally their task of assessing the schemes which came before them. I have heard critics of the RFAC claim that their verdicts are capricious and unpredictable and that consequently they have

Highgrove House in Gloucestershire. The Prince oversaw the addition of Classical details to the house. But he is not just a 'Classicist': he took a personal interest in the design of the vernacular-looking 'beehive' on the left.

Prince's Square, Glasgow. The space in front of an old stone, Classical building has been transformed into one of the few really successful shopping centres to emerge from the boom. Architect George MacKath worked with many different craftsmen to achieve an interior that suggests something of Glasgow's 'Art Nouveau' traditions.

little weight with Planning Authorities. They also detect a 'Modernist' bias, talking darkly of the 'commanding heights' which Modernists hold on the commission. And indeed alongside Lipton sits Sir Philip Dowson and Sir Philip Powell, Michael Hopkins, scarcely it is said, tribunes of the popular will and taste.

Besides, the Commission is ultimately powerless. True, it can point a finger at schemes of which it disapproves but the hoped for infamy that such publicity has brought has done little to curb bodies like the BBC from pushing ahead with their schemes just the same.

However, by stealth and persuasion as well as by judicious publicity (Lord St John of Fawsley the Chairman has the House of Lords at his disposal for his anathemas), the Commissioners can claim to have scored many successes for the public good. But they are not, nor do they seek to be, an infallible source of aesthetic advice. Their role is judicial and if they would like a little more recognition of their existence (and the appointment of Lord St John was surely a move calculated to get it) I doubt if they would seek much extension to their powers; they don't want to become another storm centre on the architectural battlefront.

One place Lipton is less likely to go for advice is the RIBA. By its many events and the multiplicity of awards, especially the Royal Gold Medal, the RIBA does give endorsement and approval and sets standards – however confusing they may be. But torn by its own internal politics, bedevilled by chronic financial pressures, split over issues like regionalism and what to do with its library and drawings collection, the RIBA might be excused from being a fountainhead of inspiration.

Its critics would say that it is supremely ill-fitted to be so, as it too is a block house of Modernism; its HQ in Great Portland Street a citadel of the profession that according to the Prince revolutionised itself in the 50s and 60s, and deliberately turned its back on its own past and traditions.

Despite all the buffets and squalls of the last ten years which the profession has had to meet, the RIBA has more or less held the Modernist line. The last President Rod Hackney may have shared the Prince's views to a dismaying extent, but the new President Max Hutchinson was elected because he so clearly didn't agree with the Prince at all. Hutchinson has arrived at Great Portland Street as if he'd been sent for. Gone are the days when Presidents wanly welcomed the 'opening up' of the debate by the Prince. Not after *A Vision of Britain*; there'd been quite enough of this sort of thing and Hutchinson has come – if not to put a stop to it – at least to proclaim the architect's cause with vigour. Hutchinson's inaugural speech and his forthcoming book take on the Prince directly. Revealingly, the book's cover displays a picture of the subject, not the author, of the book; in fact it looks at a glance, as if it *is* the Prince's book.

Hutchinson has no time at all for an architecture which seeks to charm by its surface appearance – what he calls unappealingly 'Bimbo' architecture. He seems unimpressed by the fact that many people like or dislike a building because of how it looks. That it should therefore try and look pleasant or modestly seek to do little more than fit in is regarded as an evasion of its architectural duty. The virtue and integrity of a building lie within it and in how confidently it mobilises the materials and technology of its time.

To some members of the profession that he represents Hutchinson seems a little too keen to join the battle. He attacks not only the constituency for which the Prince speaks, but has failed to gauge the feelings of thoughtful architects of all shades of opinion who believe that perhaps more is required to improve our architecture than spirited rhetoric. Hutchinson's highly produced manner is not ineffective but it has not been enough to earn him entry to the moral and philosophical high ground which

Rogers and the Prince contest.

The new, aggressive RIBA stand will doubtless be supported by its allies in the architectural press who are given to publishing doleful editorials in which the reactionary forces unleashed by the Prince are blamed for the nationwide rash of what they wearisomely call 'Noddy' architecture and against which the dreaded accusation of 'pastiche' is monotonously levelled.

And if the architectural press see themselves as embattled defenders of the faith, the architectural schools have found themselves under attack too. The government looks with disfavour on the length of their courses and their cost, and it isn't only supporters of the Prince who see little other than irrelevant narcissism in their students' work. They have also been cast as redoubts of ideology in which students are indoctrinated and Le Corbusier is still spoken of affectionately as 'Corb' and where Mies and Gropius still retain their old prestige. Students who seek a traditional education in such places have a hard time of it. Responding to the Prince's criticisms in the film, the school's defenders claim that such things as drawing *are* taught, they say that architectural history *is* fundamental to their courses and if the students don't actually sit down and copy Corinthian capitals all day, why on earth, in 1989, should they? Like the profession, architectural education was revolutionised and put on a solid, rational basis in the 50s and 60s, breaking away from the lingering academic Classicism that until then had enfeebled our architecture.

Quite clearly architects like Quinlan Terry don't think much of the schools and John Thompson is not just speaking for himself when he said: 'I think the educational system of our profession is probably the prime cause of a lot of our problems.'

The Prince said in an interview which he gave to German television: 'What I think has gone wrong over these last 40 years is that we have abandoned the fundamental principles by which architecture has always been taught over thousands of years. If you abandon the traditional principles like teaching measured drawing, life drawing, things like having students apprenticed to craftsmen so that they learn about the actual business of how to keep a building together . . . anything goes. There's an obsession with novelty and constant change.' He *does* believe in the virtue of copying the way a shadow is cast by an antique capital over its column.

The school's apologists contend that their graduates number some of the most famous and respected architects in the world. It is only here, in philistine Britain, that their genius is not only unacknowledged but disputed and vilified.

Both sides look hopefully for 'young' architects to emerge from the schools who will add lustre to their cause. And indeed there is a crop of new designers, who are made much of by magazines like *Blueprint* but whose contributions have as yet been largely limited to the design of fashionable cafés and brasseries in the West End or exotic shops in Knightsbridge.

Practices who've developed more in the mainstream and are gaining reputations for pragmatic inventiveness, like Allies Morrison and Troughton McAslam, don't find the going easy: Troughton McAslam have completed a building in Stockley Park with which Lipton is delighted but it's difficult for a newly established firm to compete for the big jobs. So though Troughton McAslam have won a slice of the action at Canary Wharf, it is only a slice. The great developments require services and back-up that only a very few architectural practices can mobilise. However genuine the search for new, inventive architects, developers are likely to stick with the big names that give reassurance that the job can be done efficiently and on time.

A Classicist like John Simpson is a different sort of promising architect. The Prince has championed Simpson's alternative to the Arup scheme for Paternoster Square. Lipton says you can avoid the danger of monolithic design too crushingly 'master planned' by inviting architects of the brilliance and individuality of Michael Hopkins and Richard MacCormac to contribute to schemes like Sir Philip Dowson's. It is unlikely that Simpson will be invited to make a major contribution to the master plan; rather he is playing for higher stakes – a takeover of the whole project, a prospect that might not be impossible given a change of heart somewhere amidst the complicated changes of ownership that attend the site.

The big schemes like Paternoster Square bring with them a sense of excitement and the feeling that things are on the move again, that London has become the centre of the great debate which is, after all, being fought all over the world. But there is also insecurity which can generate a kind of unhelpful aggressiveness.

One of the oddest features of Max Hutchinson's inaugural speech was his attack on Terry Farrell and the Post-Modernism he was said to exemplify. Farrell might reflect that the works of Hutchinson are not of such quality as to give him the right to dismiss so thoughtful and inventive an architect as himself. Farrell is well known for his concern to try and create civilised cities but his ability to design modern buildings that cheer the place up a bit inspires accusations of impurity from both camps. He occupies a position in the middle ground of the debate and is making an impact through the sheer size of his schemes for London Wall, Charing Cross, the South Bank and the old Chiswick Bus Yard. He applies an un-hysterical analysis to the debate but is prepared to give as good as he gets. In another BBC film, *The Battle for Paternoster Square*, he described the Modern Movement as one that had deliberately turned its back on a tradition which derived its strength from its roots in the ancient wolrds of Greece and Rome and replaced it with blank architecture with no ability to communicate. It is his attempt to create an architecture that *does* communicate again that seems to infuriate Max Hutchinson so much.

Farrell, Krier, Rogers, Dowson, all share at least a passionate sense of commitment to urban design. The latest addition to this aspect of the debate is the nervously awaited Ten Principles, or the Ten Commandments the Prince called for in his film. Prudently the Prince has eschewed the apparent arrogance of 'Commandments' and gone for a softer sounding set of basic rules upon which he optimistically hopes we can all agree, ' . . . in order to provide the kind of environment that people can respond to. We need a code which reinstitutes such things as hierarchy, so that people know where the front door is, whether it's a public or private building, so that there is variety and harmony, and human scale is appreciated, not sacrificed to the machine.'

The principles will receive considerable attention and scrutiny, not necessarily hostile. Codes have a long and venerable tradition; in the past they were responsible for creating some the world's most beautiful cities. Krier will bear the Prince's rubrics in mind as he prepares his master plan. The code for building there, which he will pass on to the builders and architects who follow him, will be a local refinement of the Ten Principles. Seaside, the town in Florida on which Krier worked, has a very elaborate and sophisticated code. Lipton's Stockley Park has a code. Broadgate exemplifies all sorts of rules. The Royal Town Planning Institute welcomed the original call for 'Ten Commandments', so there is every possibility that they will be taken seriously. It may be hard for architects to muster counter arguments (Hutchinson has already dismissed them unseen) other than those based on the inviolability of their own artistic autonomy.

The Prince has already called for a return of art and craftsmanship into architecture, so it seems safe to bet that they have become 'principles'. Here too he is voicing a desire shared by many, for decoration and art to return to the built environment, from which they were banished by the stern diktats of the prophets of Modernism.

Peter Palumbo promises that there will be lots of art at No 1 Poultry. He has made art and architecture one of his main concerns as he takes over the chairmanship of the Arts Council where already a 'per cent for art' committee, under the chairmanship of the unassailably modern architect Richard Burton, is already deliberating over ways to get things moving. The Art and Architecture Group (of which I am chairman) give a continuing platform to the cause for which they have been pushing with increasing success since 1982.

Lipton has commissioned art at Stockley Park and at Broadgate where the most spectacular item is a 'controversial' iron structure of enormous height by American sculptor Richerd Serra. The most lavish windfall for public art is the £6 million which the developers of County Hall have come up with. All over the country local authorities are stumping up for art even as they cut services and close schools. So much is now expected of art's capacity not just to adorn but to transform and rgenerate that conferences are held about it, political parties find it prudent to talk about it respectfully, and the government has sponsored a book on it.

And yet how many modern buildings actually have art integrated into their design rather than stuck on just before completion? How is it that key buildings like the new Design Museum bear so little evidence in their construction of the hand of the artist or craftsman?

And what kind of art will the suddenly available millions promote? The Arts Council itself is not indifferent to a possible Eldorado for the visual arts in a culture traditionally weighted towards literature and the performing arts, and are available, as are various expert agencies around the country, to give a guiding hand to developers, local authorities and architects who might, through naivety, spend the money on the wrong sort of art.

People like Krier argue that this merely extends the role and grip of professional experts who since the war have made such a disastrous mess of things anyway; foisting their own idea of what is correct and appropriate onto everybody else. Krier believes it is necessary for us to develop confidence in our own tastes and judgements so that the expert advice of the committees and coteries can be tested and if necessary rejected. Krier condemns with special vehemence the 'per cent for art' idea which he says is likely to spawn inevitably horrible art as it is generated by the same base and ignoble motives that inspired the building. Krier seems to argue that public art is impossible, until society itself has found its path again. How *can* you have public art when society has lost the ability to make judgements about what is good and what is bad? These are councils of perfection. Should we hold aloof from voting in an imperfect democracy – until politicians emerge of the stature of Jefferson or Pitt the Younger?

And decoration is not just about the trivial adornment of a building. Much of what the Prince objected to in architecture was to do with scale. Sir Roy Strong made a comparison between the great medieval cathedrals and Cesar Pelli's gigantic tower at Canary Wharf in the Prince's film. Architect Robert Adam remarked at an Academy Editions seminar following the film that cathedrals were indeed massive in scale. But their scale was made human and accessible by the wealth of their detail, the complexity of their surface. Modernism abandoned detail. Much hangs upon the way Sir Roy Strong mobilises art and craftmanship at Canary Wharf.

Some of the Prince's critics question not only his principles but his right to express controversial views at all. He is reputedly surrounded by a cabal of sinister, undemocratically elected advisers. Moreover he is, they say, intruding unconstitutionally on the planning system which, though of Byzantine complexity, it is the best we have and is, for all its faults, democratic. Their accusation seems to be that a note of disapproval from him will distort all proceedings and findings and make those involved in the planning process abandon any sense of personal judgement. By such an argument it was only the fact that the inspectors' report on No 1 Poultry was written before the film containing the famous '1930s wireless' remark was shown, that prevented the Mappin and Webb building from being saved. (Mr Ridley's endorsement of the report came much later but he proved himself capable of exercising his democratic duties.) Nonetheless the critics would like to see the Prince return to opening factories. Disappointingly for them the Prince indicated in the same television interview that this is not to be. He acknowledges the dangers '. . . if you step outside the conventional limitations someone like myself is said to operate under. But I felt actually very strongly with architectural and environmental matters that these were areas which I sensed were above party politics and fairly safe for me to step into. Of course those who don't like what I say will want me to keep my mouth shut or keep to uttering platitudinous remarks. I think life is more important than that. I'm one of those people who mind; probably too much about some things. I mind very much about the environment.'

Most building activity in the environment of which he speaks is concerned less with shining new visions than with alterations to exisiting buildings, refurbishment and conservation. And for all the energy of the debate, squalor and dirt still blight enormous areas of the country. What Rogers likes to call 'the public realm' has been impoverished by public and government neglect. The streets are clogged with litter as well as choked with traffic. Urban and rural life is under terrific strain.

Style is not irrelevent to issues like these. But is it schizophrenia or the vigorous self-confidence of a society cheerfully having it both ways that can simultaneously produce Lloyd's and Richmond Riverside, the Arups and the John Simpson schemes for Paternoster Square?

And is it possible to include in the debate alternatives to the extremes? There is much more complexity in the arguments of the protagonists than those in the media, who hold the ring to the debate, are usually prepared to grant them.

It is a misinterpretation of the Prince's vews to say that he wishes merely to return to the past. It is a misinterpretation of Rogers to suggest that he wishes to cover the country with buildings like Lloyd's. If 'plurality' doesn't sound quite like a call to arms to architects used to the hard-edged certainties of Modernism, it is, nonetheless, an idea that should flourish – not wither in a democracy. Krier speaks of the need for getting together with people you respect and then respecting their rights of freedom of expression, freedom of thought, freedom of style. After all, the original impetus of the Modern Movement was hopeful and open.

Dorchester, Stockley Park, the new Kings Cross give some idea of the plurality that the country's architecture now offers. Within that, the public is entitled to hope that decent, humane architecture will emerge from the conflicting visions, that the 'second chance' will produce architecture that responds to our needs for variety and beauty and will be inspired by things other than financial expediency and arrogance. Perhaps it will be shaped by the demands of energy conservation and pressures that are environmental in an ecological sense, that insist that technology must be used as responsibly in towns and cities as in estuaries, forests, lakes and mountains: and manipulated within the urban landscape with as much sensitivity and creativity as in the countryside. Richard Rogers calls for a new ethic, equal to the exhilerating possibilities that technology opens to a democracy confident enough to take them.

The Prince calls for a return to a much older ethic. On the disputed territory between them most people would welcome the return of an architecture that has soul and is inspired by ethical considerations. For that to happen the impulse is likely to come not from rhetoric but the common sense instincts of the heart.

But what Robert Adam calls the revolutionary view of history, the avant garde, the supremacy of technology, still keeps its grip on many imaginations. There are many interesting battles yet to be fought.

Knocking down the past: HRH The Prince of Wales lends a hand to the task of demolishing a 60's car park at Bow in East London. Enjoyable work but, as he said, perhaps symbolically, 'harder than it looks'.

CHARLES JENCKS
Prince Charles Joins the Architectural Debate.

PRINCE CHARLES, FROM A VISION OF BRITAIN

Prince Charles' controversial forays into the architectural battlefield, culminating in a book and exhibition at the V&A have certainly brought architecture to public attention. The Tate symposium, organised in 1988 by the Academy Forum, created a platform for critics and architects to discuss issues arising from these interventions. Papers by Michael Manser and Anthony Sampson are published here, with an essay by Charles Jencks, and statements by Krier, Porphyrios etc.

Whatever we may think of the Prince's views on architecture, whether he is the 'conscience of the nation' or 'ill-informed', we should note some important points that are often missed. He has created a national debate on architecture where before there were small-scale professional disputes, and he has spoken out with considerable pleasure, even an unguarded zest. His constant squibs, his 'monstrous carbuncles' and 'glass stumps' indicate this enjoyment, as much as his mixed metaphors.

There is a humour latent in these 'royal bricks' smashing through 'professional plate glass' to stir up the 'spaghetti bolognese of red tape' which should remind us that his interventions are tentative, that he has asked for a debate not a *diktat* on architecture and that the very real pluralist situation allows the five or six different approaches to architecture to continue flourishing. In the heat of debate we have lost sight of this very real accomplishment of the last ten years: we are closer now than we have been for 70 years to welcoming different schools and philosophies of architecture and to judging any style or approach with respect to its context and function. In short, pluralism, not the profession of architects nor the Prince, reigns in Britain.

This pluralism is, as far as I'm concerned, to be supported and protected against all those who would close down the debate, or limit architecture to the tastes of a profession or an elite. And in the contentious taste wars of the present there are indeed many who wish to return to architecture that is a closed shop with a single orthodoxy. Just as Norman Tebbit sent what was construed as a shot across Prince Charles' bow, warning him to steer clear of politics, so many architects and critics have sent

threatening letters and unguided missiles across his path, effectively saying that those who live in 18th-century stone houses shouldn't throw bricks – that royals should leave the style wars to architects. This would be, in my view, a typical reactionary position. The Prince's interventions in architecture have, so far, widened the scope of debate, increased pluralism and the minorities, and they should be supported until this ceases to be the case.

It is time to move on to a new stage. The profession, like most of the country, now acknowledges the problems with the old-type Modernism and the stupidity of destroying historic centres. There probably isn't an architect alive who would propose the tower block solutions of Ronan Point, or the City in the Park of Le Corbusier. These are ducks which can be pronounced moribund and there's no point, to mix a metaphor, in flogging dead birds. We must move beyond the polarisations and arguments of the 1970s. The Prince's interventions on architecture have increased the public visibility of the profession. Now an expansion of taste is necessary; he must deepen his involvement with architecture and expand his range of advisers. The pluralism of present architecture directly reflects the different taste-cultures of the public and no single style or approach is adequate for the country as a whole, or should dominate the profession. If this is right then the next stage of debate will concern quality and discrimination. We might give up attacking and supporting styles of architecture in their entirety and discriminate within a genre, and judge how appropriate it is to any particular context. Then the debate, and style wars of 20 years, will start to get interesting and fruitful.

MICHAEL MANSER
The Prince and the Architects

MANSER ASSOCIATES, HEATHROW HOTEL, MODEL

Hampton Court, May 29th 1984, was the place and the time of the first tirade against Modern architecture by the Prince of Wales. He made it while presenting the Gold Medal for Architecture on behalf of the Queen to Indian architect Charles Correa. The year was the 150th anniversary of the RIBA and was being celebrated by a 1000-event Festival of Architecture of which the Royal Gold Medal ceremony had been made a key event. Although

billed by the press as a self-congratulatory party (and surely the last 150 years have spawned enough major architectural monuments to justify self-congratulation), the central figure of the evening was Charles Correa; generously recommended to the Queen by the RIBA in its own anniversary year for, amongst other work, his achievements in low-cost housing for the truly deprived.

It had been thought the Prince would enter into the spirit of the evening and make a supportive speech and in particular would show interest in Correa's work in India. A small exhibition had been arranged, the Aga Khan had provided Indian celebratory wreaths for the Prince and Correa, a masque had been commissioned for the occasion – the first since the 18th century – and there were 700 guests, the majority of whom were not architects. There was a candlelit dinner in the State Apartments and at the end a spectacular firework display over the Grand Canal. It was the largest party ever held at Hampton Court and afterwards the Lord Chamberlain's office commented that only architects would have had the genius to think of lighting the State Apartments by candles alone!

Hundreds of people had spent months preparing for the evening – a joyous festival – to fete the anniversary Gold Medallist, Charles Correa. In the event he lost his central role. Transcripts of the Prince's speech had been sent to *The Times* and the *Guardian* during the afternoon and the *Guardian* forwarded it to the RIBA. Its contents caused consternation and dismay. Attempts made through the Palace to persuade the Prince to make a different speech were to no avail and, standing

beside me, he delivered it to a startled audience and delighted TV crews who, alerted by the leaked speech, had attended in unexpected numbers. As he finished the Prince turned to me and said with a wry expression, 'I'm sorry about that.'

I contemplated countering his point of view then and there but to do so would have turned a spoilt event into a disaster. As Penny Junor said in a subsequent biography of the Prince of Wales, 'It was misjudged if not downright rude'. On the plus side the Prince that evening set up a discussion and interest in architecture not known since the 19th century. For me that alone did much to balance the right or wrongs of the evening at Hampton Court. What has happened since is another matter. Under the Prince's relentlessly biased attack the discussion has degenerated into a depressingly negative 'old versus new'. Because of the Prince's enormous influence, architecture other than the kind believed to be admired by the Prince is out of favour and there is a growing censorship against modernity. It is true that during the 1950s and 60s architects who pursued other than what was then known as the Modern Movement were regarded as renegades by their colleagues. Perhaps that was bad. But it was an interprofessional prejudice and had little influence on the public, so a variety of architecture was built.

Nothing was actually lost; the loss at the moment is architecture truly reflecting the aspirations and needs of our time, built in contemporary techniques and materials. Each generation needs to create its new and unfamiliar architecture. Without this constant evolution there can be no heritage for the future. Mistakes are inevitably made, that is the risk of experiment, but

in the past there was a tradition of replacing or remodelling obsolete buildings – a practice central to organic urban growth – but now resisted by a nostalgic society led by a nostalgic Prince.

William Morris was, in the 19th century, the founder of the Society for the Protection of Ancient Buildings. By today's standards his view of ancient buildings was very uncertain. In his words, 'the 18th century was quite unconscious of its tendency toward ugliness and nullity', the houses of that period he concedes as having been 'built solidly and conscientiously, at best, and if they have little or no beauty, yet they are at the worst not agressively ugly or base and it is possible to live in them without serious disturbance to our work or thoughts.'

Morris was no more charitable about his near contemporaries Paxton, Brunel, Burton and Turner, whose work he wrote off as 'the horrible and restless nightmare of modern engineering'. William Morris was a sensitive and creative man, highly regarded and respected in his time. A man of the arts. Supposing he had survived to become a listing officer in the Department of the Environment, a Town Planner Committee chairman or a Planning Officer?

Maupassant, another literary figure, was said to have fled screaming from the sight of the Eiffel Tower saying that he could not endure its colossal vulgarity. Morris, during his visit to Paris, spent most of his days in the Tower reading and writing. To a French friend who said how pleased he was that he liked the Tower, Morris answered, 'Like it, it is the only place in Paris where I can avoid seeing the damn thing.' Over the passage of time the Eiffel Tower has become the popular symbol of Paris. There would be a great outcry from conservation societies if such a construction was proposed today; and of course exactly the same people would protest the loudest if it was proposed to demolish the present Tower.

A follow-on from unscholarly conservation is the 'In Keeping' policies. Never was there a more absurd architectural idea; an idea totally unsupported by history and ironically enough the very reason why William Morris started the society for the Preservation of Ancient Buildings was because he was appalled by the 'In Keeping' restoration of Tewkesbury Cathedral by Gilbert Scott. He thought such activity demeaned a great building, which it does. Restoring old work is one thing, faking-in new additions is quite another.

Built communities have evolved, generation by generation, as a series of perceivable steps in time. Because buildings were originally for economic reasons built from materials close to

hand, there were regional characteristics of materials but these did not particularly influence style or scale. There was little sentiment about earlier buildings and if they were useful they survived and if they were loved and thought beautiful they also survived. If not they were demolished and the materials re-used. There was no notion that buildings should be in keeping with those built earlier, or that tall buildings should not be built alongside small buildings. Townscapes formed organically step by step and the steps varied in size from a single small house to whole squares and terraces and major public buildings. Above all, those who built in the past had huge confidence in their own times and what they were doing.

How many great works of architecture and townscape of the past would have been allowed if present attitudes had then prevailed? Would Nash have been allowed to remodel St James' Palace? Would Inigo Jones have been allowed to disfigure the burnt-out remains of medieval Wilton House with his strident Renaissance reconstruction? And Wren's wrecking of Cardinal Wolsey's soft plum-coloured brick Hampton Court with his vulgar orange and white extensions bashed in without care of in-keeping, conformity or respect? And the skyline of London wrecked by all those spires and that gross mountain of St Paul's?

The crowning argument for letting current designers pursue their contemporary conviction is that contemporary criticism is invariably later shown to be wayward and capricious, as was that of William Morris and Balzac. Old buildings become imbued after the passage of time with qualities of nostalgia, familiarity, tradition and permanence of background which has little to do with architectural quality. Each phase of architectural development falls into fashionable disrepute shortly after it becomes reasonably established. Between the wars architectural theorists were scathing about Victorian revivalism; now we have the Victorian Society and a more generous view of Victorian architecture. After the last war it was the 30s which were viewed with contempt. The Festival of Britain and the International Modern Style which had been brewing up was the good news. Now in the last few years we have had a 1930s exhibition in London and Lutyens, who the bright young things of the late 30s, 40s and 50s thought was a total reactionary, has been declared the very greatest. In 15 years there will certainly be a huge revival of interest in Basil Spence – the last Romantic and the first to show High-Tech tendencies.

The Trafalgar Square National Gallery competition exhibition invited visitors, the public, to vote for their preference of the

sary. It was unfortunate that the Prince did not feel able to go for the larger question of the role of developers and the commercial problems which, to my view, have been responsible for far greater damage to the skyline of London and to the whole aspect of British architecture.

Commercial incentives which do not have any architectural inspiration behind them, are far more dangerous than the most daring kind of architecture, whatever you may think of it, because something like the skyline along the Thames had no architectural interest whatsoever, it was a purely commercially-inspired development for the most mean and boring motives. I think it is a pity that the Prince didn't feel able to launch into that area. It may be that he did not feel he could do so without becoming more political because he would be discussing the nature of Capitalism by doing so. Any argument about architecture which does not include a discussion of the whole relationship with developers and big money is a bogus one. I don't say is as a Marxist, or indeed as an anti-Capitalist, but I think that to pretend that architecture is a pure profession and that it doesn't have those commercial pressures, is pure humbug, and to simply set one style against another without talking about money is absurd.

I think that the Prince's attack was bound to be unfair in a way. Very likely, he himself did not fully understand the astonishing mystique of the monarchy and the inhibitions that people have about discussing or criticising what he says, even though he himself said that he would welcome a debate. A recent book revealed that half the people in Britain have dreams about the Queen. This clearly suggests that any discussion about the monarchy must have a strong subconscious element which it is difficult to fully exorcise. But even apart from the more subconscious side, there remains the element of concern that if you are going to support things that the Prince might not like, this will somehow damage your career and that it will have effects in terms of not getting knighthoods or not being received in the best circles and so on. There is this very definite emotional, irrational element as well as the more rational one that some people have undoubtedly lost some business as a result of what was said. So I think that in those ways the criticism has been unfair, although one cannot say that it is unconstitutional because the constitution is undoubtedly extremely vague on this issue.

This brings me to what we might be able to do to best take advantage of this situation, because I think that it would be a great mistake for us, either the interested public or the architects, to say that the thing for us to do is to shut up. What is clear is that the argument has to be a pretty robust one. I don't think there is any point in concealing the nature of people's feelings. Above all, it is essential for the architects themselves to become much more politically aware, much tougher and much more prepared to attack each other. That, of course, is the essential problem with all professions, including my own, that they will always tend to rally round over certain elements when attacked from the outside, whereas, of course, their credibility and their general relationship with the public depends on their being seen to air out every issue themselves, before they are attacked from the outside.

I think, to some extent, it has to be personal, in terms of what the Prince's role should be. For instance, when he compares himself to the Prince Consort, it is a very interesting comparison,

but one has to point out that the Prince Consort was much more actively involved in actual contemporary building in his time and took a more positive interest in architecture. It is an absolutely essential element in any argument about any subject, that at some point or other you must say to the other person, 'Well what will you do better? What do you actually want?' You simply cannot attack everything that is new.

When you look at what is happening today in London, particularly when you look at the docklands, the ordinary public, and I am sure the architects too, almost every day, will suddenly notice a building which they never thought was going up at all, which has suddenly emerged. The feeling is that the skyline of London is somehow being changed without anybody really discussing what sort of city it should be. Of course, docklands is the most astonishing example of this because it has virtually no limitations in terms of planning and we suddenly wake up to find a new city at our doors with some of the most astonishing mixtures of architecture that I can imagine in a city anywhere in the world. That kind of debate, about what kind of architecture we are going to have, can only be originated by the architects themselves, and only by bringing that out in the open will the public become interested and more supportive of what they are trying to do. But it must be a candid one, about the nature of commercial pressure and what can be done by architects to limit or improve this.

Finally, I would suggest that a large part of the solution will lie not with a purely domestic discussion, because so much of the real excitement and the real importance of architecture, particularly in the Modern and Post-Modern movements, is international. What is happening very rapidly, as well as the whole debate about communal and more local building, is the extent to which exciting architecture is becoming a very competitive business across the world, in which the world's cities, the financial cities particularly, are competing with each other though exciting new buildings which are measuring themselves against each other. It is from there that so much of the most thrilling building is coming. But it is no accident, it seems to me, that some of the architects who appear to be most attacked in Britain are those that do most business internationally and are a part of an enormously vibrant international movement. I think now that we are in a new age, with many of us flying a great deal across the world, this element of competition between really enterprising and thrilling buildings becomes far more important. The equivalent to the old architectural competition that one saw on the Grand Canal with competing corporations trying to outbid each other in boldness of architecture, is now to be seen across the continents; the newest buildings in Hong Kong, New York and very often the Far East, compete in terms of grandeur and self-respect to show what their countries can do.

To escape from the parochialism and what I say is traditional Philistinism of the British attitude towards architecture, and perhaps escape a bit from this sort of family quarrel we are caught up in with our monarchy, the more the architects and the public can look at architecture in that international context as well as the local one, the more healthy the debate will become and the more I think we will be able to give credit to exciting and innovative architecture, as well as maintaining the element of common or sane architecture for ordinary, simple people's lives.

DISCUSSION

The following statements formed part of the Tate discussion in which leading architects and critics responded to the controversial issues raised by the papers, above all revealing the diversity of opinion concerning the Prince's role in the architectural debate.

I do hope that because the monarchy has a problem finding an identity for itself, we are not going to allow the monarchy a role by default – because there is no other role for them, we will allow them a voice. The monarchy, the aristocracy, like criminals, like lunatics, do not vote. Not voting seems to suggest that there is something in our structure which says we will not give you the right of speech, we do not want a spokesman to come out of those three groups. I feel that the issue here – if we're going to talk about that – should not be 'Do we like modern architecture?', 'Do we like neo-vernacular?', but what is the role of a member of the monarchy today? Do they have a role in opinion-making in our society?

Stephen Games

One aspect we haven't touched on which I think is quite profound for architects, is the problem of public language, and a language in which to be able to express other things than purely commercial activities. Now for several millenia, this architecture performed a secondary role, while its primary role was to express those transitory moments of man's life – birth, marriage, death – and to celebrate and to concretise his institutions through which he first found expression. For a number of years – since the Modern Movement – we have not only found it very difficult to make monuments, we found it almost immoral to do so or to even try. Feelings of nationhood, inheritance, piety, religion, are very real emotions, and I believe there is a real demand to express them and I believe the implication of the Prince's speech is that he recognises these are important themes which the man in the street wants to be able to express. The modern architect has ignored them, and we must now address ourselves to this need and find a language in which we can do this. It may be that buildings are commercial, but I believe that there is a language through which we can also express other things – we can fill the function of commercialism but also say something more.

John Melvin

The role that the Prince is filling is, I think, a very real one, and I don't see that from a constitutional point of view there is any justification in criticising him for doing so. That having happened, we are now faced with some very real difficulties, and some very real dangers arising out of what he did. Because of his role the debate can no longer be a purely public debate. Something very insidious is happening, because he is being used in the continuing process of the debate that he started. He is being used by architects who want to filter through their own individual and personal views; he is being used by developers who dare not expose what they want to do to the public, but fear that they are going to be condemned by him, or treat him as some new tier of planning authority to get through. So what is actually happening is paradoxically quite the opposite of the public debate that I am sure he intended to start. We have not got the proper forum to hold this public debate. The planning system is not a proper forum. I think the one thing that we should really address now is whether we take Michael Manser's view that effectively experience of the past tells us that you get the best architecture with very, very little control. You just allow things to happen, and by and large they will happen right, and things that aren't right won't stand the test of time, and we'll all look back at it with a

broader, more objective view than we had at the time. Or if we say we are living in an age when we do have to have controls, we need to have ways of ensuring that our architecture can fit in, that the community does balance against the development of the environment. But we also have got to create some new forum for this debate about architecture as opposed to debates about planning, conservation or development of the environment.

David Michael

I think the Prince is in a frightfully unenviable position, and it's going to get worse. By media manipulation more than anything else, he has been landed with the whole role in society that an aristocracy should carry. By aristocracy, I don't mean necessarily members of the House of Lords, I mean, a fully informed, debated, articulate society with a sense of responsibility to everybody else. And the other thing I would like you to consider is the rise, the florescence and the decline of the collective in political structures since 1860. It rose to an eminence in all its different guises between 1900 and 1970 and now it is heavily in decline, so that the collective has a battle going on which it still operates in the commercial repercussions of anonymity. This is what must be attacked next.

Patrick Nuttgens

I feel that both Charles Jencks and Michael Manser have assisted what seems to me to be the exact point of this debate, which is not about stylistics. It is not a debate say between Modernism and Post-Modernism, between Gothicism and Empire Style, but it is a debate between traditional architecture and modern architecture, and in that sense I think the comments and criticism of Prince Charles have to do with planning, with urban design, with the definition of the plot, the establishment of the city as opposed to the destruction of the city, in other words with urban design issues, rather than stylistic issues.

Demetri Porphyrios

Historically, if you look at the 80s and look at what is the architecture of the period, the bulk of the buildings produced in this country are neo-vernacular and that is a creation of the planning system. The architectural profession has tried to pretend that the planning system isn't there, hoping that it will go away. The truth is it won't and it's an issue that we have to deal with, we have to live through this system of control and that is one of the major factors which produces the architecture of today. Well, I hope the Prince of Wales, by effectively acting like a super chairman of a planning committee, may bring home the fact that these controls will not go away. We have to reconcile ourselves to them and deal with them by reproducing buildings of today which are not buildings that belong to philosophies of the 60s.

Robert Adam

I would like to remove the monarchy from the situation and look at the reality, because there are comparisons internationally where broadly speaking there are no monarchies. The filters which society provides through its bureaucracies, its conventions, its limitations, its absence or presence of culture, express dramatically and clearly the architecture which is allowed in a given context. The public, by definition, use and see everyday what there is to be used and seen in the way of architecture. The real problem is the increase in the sheer pace of building, the tremendous population increase, the effect of the motor car, the effect of the motorway, the effect of aircraft, and the reduction of the globe in dramatic terms.

Jake Brown

I think we are generally agreed that Prince Charles is very good for speaking out for the common man on modern architecture. But on the other hand, he hasn't got a clue about the profession. If you wander around Britain with your eyes open, what distinguishes the better towns, the earlier towns, is their enormous variety. What makes the New Towns rather boring is their conformity. Bath is exquisite, but if it was continuous right across Britain, it would be very trying.

Michael Manser

I must say that the Prince of Wales' speaking aloud is, I think, really most vital, holding the mirror to the architects and professionals who have forced such a mess on this country. They had a free reign for 40 years, they built plenty of new homes, they had no controls, they could do what they wanted, they experimented their theories, and it has all created an unholy mess. Now if you were a young prince, driving around the country and seeing what's happening to it, you would understand why the man is alarmed. The architects always put the blame for the mess on to the developers. The developers put it on to the planners, the planners put it onto the architects, and so on. I think the problem is very much to do with the architects because the conformity which you were blaming on the British public, is actually another conformity which provides the architectural schools where nothing else but making boxes is taught. There was been no teacher of *architecture* in architectural schools for 30 years, and anyone like Raymond Erith who tried to do that would be thrown out – Raymond Erith was not asked to design a New Town, not even a pub or a square. His way was considered not to be the right way to design, because architects thought they had the new model, the way to build the new Jerusalem.

Obviously a sovereign, who has an interest in his country, has to speak out. If he has intelligence, perception and humanity, he must cry out the way he does. And of course, being so much in the public eye, he will be terribly criticised by those who are responsible for it. Indeed, the architects, planners and developers don't like it; they try to tease him now, but that's a way of showing contempt for the values he stands for. The man flies aeroplanes, he loves modern technology where it applies, where, it is reasonable, but not in the house. The idea of the house has not been revolutionised by Einstein. So the house is a home, which is long term, and the city is a theme, which is a long-term subject. He speaks out for the common interest and the common good; I think that's much bigger than the common man. And that is, I think, what will possibly be able to change the climate within the architectural profession, the crisis which reigns there now. Michael Manser says conservation has gone too far. If you drive across London, avoiding the nice parks, you see that London, like no other city in the world, is destroyed, having been a very nice city. So I think that all this will lead to a very profound debate – so we see what architecture is about, what the form of a city should be. Suddenly the developers of St Paul's have cut down to one half the amount of offices they had to build six months ago. How did all this happen? Just because the Prince said a word, something was obviously not necessary, the pressure was fictitious. There is a leadership in the profession which does not take the moral, rational spirit it needs, to debate what the issues of architecture are: is it just to build offices any size?

What is the density? What should they look like? Are they built for longer terms? I think the Prince, like no one else, addresses these public issues, and you should be grateful.

Leon Krier

One thing that excited me about the 1984 speech by the Prince was that I thought it was going to trigger the big debate that we have been waiting for. Much to my disappointment, architects, being romantic, took it with such masochistic ecstasy that it defeated its own purpose. He got us into the light of the media and there's an important intellectual debate to be presented to the public, and unfortunately what is being presented to the public is all these interesting phrases that magazines can cut up and paste. If there is anything that represents British architecture to me it is eclecticism and now we are in an era that is going into the new vernacular, and has an enormous field to explore. Maybe the élitism of taste and what the architect likes is a threat to that wonderful eclecticism.

Sama Farati

I can't see how the architectural profession, never mind the individual architects trying to do buildings in the city for instance, can argue with this god-like creature. And it seems to me extremely serious that one throw-away word can destroy years of work by qualified professionals who are trying to do the best they can for a particular situation. So that somehow, the profession has to face up to this, that they are now up against something which is almost beyond them.

Richard Hughes

I think basically what we discuss here is criticism. I don't think it's just architecture that Prince Charles has attacked; it is the untouchable professions in this country, keeping their expertise to themselves, whether it's the medical world or architecture, or whether it's the art world as such. No outsider who isn't a part of the society is allowed to comment on it . . . I pity you in a way, because it must be very hard facing articulate non-experts who really think and feel that they have the right to criticise and comment, and can't any longer be shut up.

Karen Phillips

What I find most depressing about the British scene – and many people brought it up – is the anonymity, the fact that nobody knows who those buildings at that skyline at the Thames belong to, who they were built for, what they represent. Whereas, the exciting buildings generally, whether in New York or London or Germany, are ones that you identify, you know who to blame if it's bad, and if it's good you know who to praise. And it is striking that with the Lloyd's building in London, whatever people think about it, it is absolutely clear what it was built for, and it's tremendously exciting for that reason. I was very struck in Hong Kong by the visual excitement of seeing two sensational skyscrapers, both unbelievably bold, one of them representing the international capital of Hong Kong bank, and the other representing the Bank of China which is technically a Communist bank. It's this element that I think is most missing in Britain and I think it's relevant to what we are talking about with Prince Charles, because there is a lack of robustness in the response, partly for this reason. What Prince Charles is partly responding to is this tremendous sense of anonymity, the undefined relationship between architects and developers, producing something very boring. And I think the more the argument is personalised, the more we know who we're talking about, who designed things, who they were designed for, the more robust the argument will become because we'll know who to blame and who to praise.

Anthony Sampson

CHARLES JENCKS
Ethics and Prince Charles

JAMES STIRLING, MICHAEL WILFORD & ASSOCIATES, NO 1 POULTRY, DRAWING OF BUILDING VIEWED FROM BANK

Behind Prince Charles' witty metaphors lie questions of the ethics of personal attacks and of royal intervention in the name of 'public' opinion. Charles Jencks looks at the issues behind what can be seen as a brilliant use, or abuse, of the media, and suggests an underlying moral crusade in the Prince's desire for a return to tradition. Since writing this article for the SOM Symposium, one of his targets – Stirling's scheme for No 1 Poultry – has been given planning permission.

Ethics and aesthetics are similar in three respects. They both are minority pursuits, they both require a slowly nurtured taste for making fine discriminations and they both demand a kind of love or passion. Now that business students are asking for university courses on ethics in the US, now that architects and planners are looking for ethical guidance – and some for a Modern Ten Commandments – we have an international conference, and some might say a new era of ethical concern. I hope so, but I doubt it.

A developed ethical sensibility, like the aesthetic, can be damaging to your health – or at least your career. You won't get ahead in the corporate world by asking the kind of difficult questions which ethics raise; better become a novelist, if you really care, because only in a novel can the beauty of fine ethical behaviour be illuminated in all its complexity. And yet for those who care deeply about moral behaviour the passion endures and continues to be guided by the same tenacious intelligence that is applied, say, to the most complex game of chess. We probably all have some ethical sensibility even if very few are the equivalent to Korchnoi or Karpov.

There are so many aspects of ethics and architecture that I'm going to concentrate on just two areas: a discussion of Prince Charles' most recent intervention in the architectural debate, and my defence of pluralism. Of course the subject is much wider than my reduction, but since I have only a short time and am in the land of Mies van der Rohe, you'll have to accept that 'less width is more focus'.

The Holy War

The Prince, as everyone knows who watches television and reads the papers, has been attacking Modern architects for four years. I have written an analysis of this attack, a book called *The Prince, The Architects and New Wave Monarchy*, which comes to the rather unexceptional conclusion that, on the whole, the Prince's intervention in the architectural debate has been, up to June 1988, marginally positive. He has made the debate more public, defended three minorities needing defence – Community Architecture, Classicism, Conservation (the three C's) – and started to define a new role for future royalty which is freer to intervene in public issues. I called it *New Wave Monarchy*, ironically, to bring out its Modernist agenda, the fact that the Prince is behaving very like Le Corbusier and Pablo Picasso in forcing his revolutionary message on the Establishment.

No one noticed my irony or reinterpretation of Bagehot, the 19th-century 'expert' on constitutional monarchy, since almost everyone in Britain focuses on the more partisan issue of 'whether you're for or against the Prince'. I mention this point to get it out of the way and decrease speculation: I did marginally support the Prince because he was increasing the options of architecture, and I now marginally object to his interventions because I find them reducing pluralism – and unethical as well. A fit subject for this conference.

At the moment British architects and the Prince are engaged in something of a Holy War of words. Fully armed metaphors fly about intent on vaporising the Modernist enemy for its 'glass stump' or 'incinerator', while a Royal Gold Medallist – subject to this first strike – will counter with a missile marked 'Prince Charles is like Stalin' (Berthold Lubetkin's comparison, if not exact words). The battle of epithets reached Gulf War proportions this late October with the Prince damning Sir Denys Lasdun's National Theatre as a 'nuclear power station', Colin St John Wilsons' British Library as 'an academy for the secret police', and James Stirling's proposal for the Mansion House site on Poultry Street as an 'old 1930s wireless'. This last barb was an intentional intervention in a public inquiry, a democratic process which the Prince – when it suits his taste – otherwise strongly supports. It brought the relatively muted reply from Stirling: 'I do not accept his flip comment about our design for No 1 Poultry . . . nor do I think it proper that he should – for the second time – influence the outcome of a democratic Public Inquiry process for this site'.

'Democratic . . . process', is there such a thing? The Prince's first foray into architectural criticism in 1984 was made in front of the then Environment Secretary, Patrick Jenkin, who was about to make a ruling on his inspectors' reports. On hearing the Prince's two characterisations – Mies van der Rohe's proposal as a 'glass stump' and ABK's as a 'monstrous carbuncle' – Jenkin whispered to his neighbour 'Well, that's two decisions I don't have to make' – and he quickly quashed both. Thus two words from the Prince managed to overturn an inspector's report and the supposedly objective results of an open public process.

No one could get away with such behaviour – certainly no elected official – unless he were charming, sincere, had 'ordinary people' on his side, and was a Prince. Many people, myself included, had been willing to excuse an exaggeration here or rude comment there because Prince Charles was apparently speaking for a helpless minority that had no other voice – the silent minority of council house dwellers. It's true that many others had been speaking out for these disenfranchised souls since the 1960s – the Advocacy planners, the Post-Modernists, Jane Jacobs and their counterparts in Britain – but they hadn't a *powerful* voice. And so a kind of bargain was struck.

Most architects (two-thirds of those polled in early 1988 by the widely read magazine *Building Design*) thought the Prince should keep speaking out on architecture – and were willing to excuse his overstatements – but they hoped he would widen his tastes and group of advisors. In effect, most architects, James Stirling included, agreed with his attack on ugliness and the mean-spirited development that has characterised Britain since the War: agreed because they also had been saying much the same thing for 20 years. Thus a clear opportunity existed this October when the Prince made his BBC film, *A Vision of Britain*, for a united front to be forged with the profession and a real change made in the architectural climate. Instead the Prince indulged in further Modernist-bashing, attacked architects of quality such as Philip Dowson, Colin St John Wilson, Denys Lasdun, James Stirling, let the real villains such as Richard Seifert and unscrupulous developers off the hook, and, with his royal influence, intervened in two democratic processes: the Mansion House Inquiry and the Paternoster Development north of St Paul's Cathedral.

The Prince continued to intervene unfairly and undemocratically because he claimed to have the people on his side, a claim which looks true at first. Over six million viewers watched his latest film (about five times the number that watched other programmes in the series) and, according to an unofficial poll, 75.5 per cent agreed with his thrashing of Modern buildings. His television ratings are higher than any other performer except David Attenborough of *Wildlife,* and apparently the flood of mail received after his last performance gave him near unanimous support. This was precisely what he asked for, several times in

the film: a clear indication that he 'wasn't alone in having these opinions', that he 'wasn't speaking just for myself'.

The Prince is conducting what he calls a popular 'crusade' for 'ordinary people' and he is such a fervent believer in democracy that he has said even monarchy 'can be a kind of elective institution. After all, if people don't want it, they won't have it'. His radical egalitarianism extends to supporting ethnic minorities, Pakistani and Indian communities within Britain, hiring blacks to work at Buckingham Palace and within other traditional preserves of white privilege. His attacks on Modern architects have always had a similar ethical basis. They were either justified because they expressed a populist opinion, the taste of 'ordinary people' or those of a helpless minority. Hence the strong injunction for client power, the unequivocal imperative which I, like others, find sympathetic: architects and planners he said, should 'provide what people want and not what they think people *should* want' (his emphasis).

This is a fine sentiment and ethical position, as far as I can see. Every individual, family or group should be able to live in a house, or flat, of their taste and any architect should try to determine the tastes of his or her ultimate client. There may be economic or physical constraints which hinder these goals, but in a democratic country where freedom of movement is possible, they are assumed as an underlying right.

But the Prince hasn't quite lived up to his professed goals. He will support democratic public inquiries insofar as they come up with populist decisions and a building that suits his own taste. The Stirling and Dowson proposals show how this baneful contradiction has arrived. In the case of Stirling's scheme for the Mansion House, the Prince could have spoken at the Public Inquiry, or made his views known while it was being debated by both sides for six weeks in a courtroom setting. Then the Stirling side could have answered, and challenged his view that the proposal looks 'like an old 1930s wireless'. Does it look like an Art Deco radio – and does the accuracy of a simile really matter? I find the comparison way off the mark – the scheme is much closer to previous Classical buildings than any mechanical instrument, and a good many critics and the architect himself believe it captures the spirit of its setting in a creative way.

But the ethical consideration also concerns the effect of the simile. Like the phrase 'monstrous carbuncle', it was *intended* to influence the Minister's final decision, negatively. It can't be asserted, as some have claimed, that the Prince was just expressing his own 'personal view' and that it is harmless, or an innocuous joke ('old radios are funny'). Or that 'nothing can be built in a conservation area', since the whole six weeks of inquiry was based on the supposition that appropriate new buildings *are* possible.

No, there can be no doubt the remark was intended to influence the Minister's final judgement and stop the scheme. The ultimate justification is that most 'ordinary people' would find it out of place, or like 'an old wireless', and therefore the Prince is right to use his royal mediapower in this cavalier way. In other words, *the populist ends justify the undemocratic means*; popular opinion, as gauged by this 'expert' on the people, can overturn the normal functioning of a supposedly unbiased inquiry.

One needn't be a lawyer, or philosopher of ethics, to see this contradiction. And it is very sad given the Prince's stated intentions to increase democracy and fair play. The second morally ambiguous point is equally simple. Are the Prince's views really those of the majority? Opinion polls taken right after a royal television appearance are bound to reflect the persuasiveness of the Prince rather than actual national taste, especially if there isn't a figure of equal stature to advocate other views. If sophisticated methods of measuring taste were used I believe they would show that all stylistic preferences – for traditional, vernacular, Classical, Modern, Post-Modern, Deconstructivist, or 'Other' – are minorities, even if some are much bigger than others. In short, existing taste is heterogeneous. In Britain, as elsewhere, there is a plurality of taste cultures none of which has an absolute majority – just like the political parties. And in architecture, unlike politics, the minority parties have certain democratic rights of ruling in their locale. True democracy in architecture must uphold the rights of local character against the wishes of the majority – as much as against the architectural profession.

A noteworthy aspect of the architectural Holy War is that most belligerents have appealed to democracy and the presumed tastes of those who will use or live in their buildings. This ethical position sanctions their opinion. Richard Rogers argues from the supposition that his Pompidou Centre has been, until the *Musée d'Orsay,* the most popular public building in France and that Modernism is popular; the former president of the RIBA and opponent of the Prince, Michael Manser, also points out that 'ordinary people' have been asserting their democratic rights in architecture for a long time – through elected committees and various procedures that allow 'all points of view' to flourish. Nearly everyone in the debate is a professed democrat and nearly everyone, like the Prince, presumes to know what people really want. In other words nearly everyone is involved in a contradiction (I won't say is hypocritical).

There are two good reasons for this. We haven't as yet taken sufficiently sensitive polls to determine the tastes and wishes of a locality, and architects would not be quite sure what to do with the results were they available. Both obstacles could be overcome and the fact that they aren't continues the Style Wars – indeed adds to their heat as each combatant cites the partial evidence of their popularity, or local relevance, or democratic planning procedure. In the absence of any means of measuring what the affected people actually want, the belligerents, like Presidential candidates, have a field day with the polls and the 'public good'. They all claim an ethical sanction for their style and approach, a sanction ultimately founded in a public opinion that is never measured!

There are, of course, many other partial justifications which help shore up their position and I might just mention these since legitimisation is the key issue in ethics. Some architects claim they are solving the 'programme requirements', the old Modernist justification, or 'extending tradition', the old Classicist rationale, or 'satisfying needs or environmental problems', the old Functionalist and Ecologist justification, or 'appealing to other architects and their own tastes', the old artist's plea. Each of these justifications has a large following among architects, but none of them carry very much public weight, especially in our sceptical age and fragmented society. Pluralism has meant that we tend to look at every moral explanation as self-justification and dismiss it as a subtle form of ideology. Such confusion and relativism will remain as long as we continue to use unclear means of democratic participation in design.

St Paul's Cathedral – the debate

A case in point concerns another intervention by the Prince in a key public site, the Paternoster area north of St Paul's Cathedral. Here a very complex process of public consultation was followed with every vested interest given a chance to influence the design: the Dean of St Paul's, the city planning officials, a jury who picked a winner from a closed competition, the inhabitants of the area who came to an exhibition showing two schemes, and the Prince – who was consulted by the developers both behind the scenes and formally. Since March 1987 a laborious process has been underway of quasi-democratic design and nearly everybody

who wants to be heard – including almost every architectural critic in London – has been heard. The process has been so long and convoluted with uncertainties that already the site has been sold twice: developers are not sure that democratic design pays.

The brief facts of the case are these. A consortium of developers, led by Stuart Lipton, set up a closed competition which was won by Arup Associates with Richard Rogers as a possible collaborator. The schemes of all seven competitors were shown, informally, to the Prince who, by that time, July 1987, had emerged as an unofficial but important part of the planning apparatus. Any scheme on a site as sensitive as Paternoster would need his tacit blessing – or so most wise developers might assume. I say this as one member of the jury that picked Arup's scheme; we were told of the many interested parties who would have to vet the decision and the possible public interaction at a later date. It seemed to me at the time, and subsequently, that this stage by stage process of democratic interaction was wise because it would allow most of the issues to be aired and a consensus on the significant points to be developed: density, land use, style and relation to the Cathedral.

In the event, the Prince didn't like any of the seven schemes and, through informal meetings with Leon Krier, Dan Cruickshank, John Simpson and a host of advisors, helped develop a counter-scheme. This was finally designed by John Simpson, sponsored by the *Evening Standard,* promoted by a heterogeneous group of Classicists and traditionalists and placed in opposition to the Arup's proposal.

A rather unequal horse-race was on with just two runners: the Arup's schematic, outline plan for the site and Simpson's detailed wooden model with all its Classical certainties and appealingly quaint ground plan. Arup's, led by Philip Dowson, did not show a final detailed solution partly because he was only asked for a planning idea and partly because, at this stage, he wanted to pose questions to the public – not answers. Simpson, supported by the *Evening Standard* as the Prince's favourite, scored a media victory when both schemes were shown to the public in June 1988. But since a public vote was never taken – and couldn't be because of the unequal degree of design development – each side could quite legitimately claim popular support: the Arup scheme because most people liked its basic design assumptions and the Simpson scheme because, in his private poll, most people said they preferred it to the undeveloped proposal. What a farce?

Not entirely. A quasi-democracy is better than none at all, and in this case, by November 1988 when the final Arup's design was shown, it produced a consensus on the important points. The fact that Arup's and Simpson's designs were, when finally worked up, rather similar in typology proves the consensus. And this could have only occurred with constant interaction and debate, a quasi-democratic process that went on for more than a year. Each side learned from the other and the six previous competitors; each side learned from the journalists, the public comment book and no doubt the Dean of St Paul's and the Prince. Democracy is about learning and, when it doesn't ruin architecture with compromise, it can produce fine achievements.

In this case it has led the developers and Arup's to reduce the density of building to acceptable levels with a series of small blocks which are scaled to the cathedral on one side and the commercial street on the other. Eight-storey blocks step down to four storeys as they approach Wren's building. The democratic process has led to a pleasant series of pedestrian spaces connected by a long curving arcade and a sequence of squares and small streets that give angled glimpses of the cathedral. It has led to a mixture of uses – commercial, retail and leisure – only housing is still absent. And it has also led to a complex aesthetic whole designed by three, and perhaps even four, different architects. They have adopted a general Free-Style Classicism which is appropriate to the area.

Some of these points were shared by all seven competitors and Simpson's scheme, but no other proposal has taken them as far because no other architect went through the whole painful process of consultation and modification. The Arup scheme is, I believe, a partial victory for quasi-democratic design.

It isn't a complete victory and the design isn't finished. In my view there are three aesthetic refinements still to be made. The colonnade order that ties together much of the fabric just north of the cathedral still needs tuning: the paired columns are too thin and the proportions of the superimposed voids are mixed up. They rise up in alternation – vertical, horizontal, vertical, horizontal – without relating the proportions of alternative levels. Secondly, the columnar order while it is structural and relevant to our time, unlike the Simpson application of Doric and Ionic modes, still has not made an expressive feature of its constructional joints, its capitals, bases or ties. Thirdly, the colonnade is too fractured, unlike Hawksmoor's proposal of 1711, and it doesn't pull in the existing brick Chapter House, so there is too much incident and variety right next to the cathedral.

There are other aesthetic points to be made about the other architects' work, but the main point is that we – the critics, the public, the Prince – can still make them and influence an open process of design.

What has been the Prince's role in this complex tale? Back in the autumn of 1987 he played a behind-the-scenes role, first looking at the seven proposals for Paternoster with dismay, then organising a counter-scheme which was ultimately designed by John Simpson. Evidently he didn't wish to take a public stand in supporting Simpson's scheme directly, so this role was taken on by the *Evening Standard,* and an ad hoc Paternoster Committee, but his position was widely known since it was constantly reported in the newspapers. Through his unofficial lobbying, and the arguments of Leon Krier and others, the density of the development was criticised as well as the over-emphasis on one function – office use. There were other points of criticism, such as style and the use of appropriate materials, but the lasting contribution of the Prince and his group, at this time, was in advocating lower densities and more mixed use – for these two points changed the subsequent Arup proposals in positive ways.

The next intervention by the Prince occurred in his famous Mansion House Speech of December 1987, when he attacked all seven proposals directly. It is best to use his own words, from his recent TV film in October 1988, to describe his feelings:

> A year ago, when I saw the developer's initial concept for a replacement, I must confess that I was deeply depressed. It didn't seem to rise to the occasion. This site is next to our great national cathedral – the very heart of the capital city. What place in Britain could be more important? This was something that I felt I had to speak up about.
> [Speech at Mansion House quoted] 'Surely here if anywhere, was the time and place to sacrifice some profit. If need be, for generosity of vision, for elegance, for dignity; for buildings which raise our spirits and our faith in commercial enterprise, and prove that capitalism can have a human face.'
> As I anticipated, there was rather an interesting row after I said all that. But it instantly became clear that I wasn't speaking just for myself. Since the speech, there's been an exhibition in the crypt of St Paul's. The outline scheme by Arup Associates held centre stage. The public at least managed a look in for once.

The implication of the Prince is that his intervention caused this exhibition in the crypt and the public involvement, but as far as I can remember Stuart Lipton talked about such involvement from the start, at least at our meetings in June 1987, and the Prince should get credit for furthering, not initiating, the participation. As I said, nearly everyone wants to be a good democrat. The Prince continues:

> There was another plan on display – by John Simpson, an architect, who works within the Classical tradition. His starting point was the original street pattern and his building defer to St Paul's. The public certainly seem to prefer the traditional materials and the far more human scale of Simpson's scheme.

But does the public prefer Simpson's scheme? The fact is we don't know, because the Gallup Poll and Simpson's private poll were measuring two different and unequal things: an Arup masterplan which was proposing general strategies so that the public *could* have a significant input in design choices, and the finished product of Simpson. It may be ethical for the Prince to gloss over this distinction, but it is not very fair for him to imply that the public preferred Simpson's design. Perhaps this is why he uses the phrase 'seem to prefer'.

In any case, he goes on to defend Simpson against the accusation of 'pastiche' and the idea that one can't clothe a modern office building with all its ducts and cables behind a traditional facade, and he concludes this defence with the summary: 'Well, I've looked into this, and you can'. You can house an up-to-date office behind a Neo-Georgian facade, as Quinlan Terry had just proved to the Nation with his Richmond scheme, a development that had a much publicised opening, by the Queen, several weeks earlier. Finally the Prince concludes his discussion of the Paternoster proposals with a shocking comparison:

> Paternoster Square has become central to the argument between Modernist and traditional architecture, or as I'd rather put it, it's the argument between the inhuman and the human.

Here, I believe, we have the very rare case of a statement that is unethical, or if not unethical at least un-Christian. The characterisation of Modernists, or Philip Dowson's architecture, as 'inhuman' does nothing to further the debate, or open alternatives, or engage the profession of architects with sweet reason. It is meant to outrage most architects, and to arouse partisan support, and coming from the Prince in front of six million viewers, it is, I believe, meant to seal the fate of Modernists.

The remark was made in a very specific context, after four years of attacking 'monstrous carbuncles' and 'glass stumps', and like one of these remarks it was meant to wound, if not kill. The irony is that, once again, the Prince has shot without aiming. He hadn't actually seen Philip Dowson's final scheme, which emerged two weeks later, and had he asked for a preview he would have found it to be Free-Style Classical and even 'human'.

His oversight, or overkill, reminds me of his apologies to the architects of the so-called 'monstrous carbuncle'. When he met them in private, and found them pleasantly human, he said "I'm sorry it had to be you.' They replied 'We're sorry it had to be you.' It has been said, and not denied, that the Prince mistook Richard Rogers' scheme for ABK's 'carbuncle', but whatever the truth of this – and the Prince has only said he was 'sorry' – it resulted in ABK losing commissions for 18 months. Such is the power of royal metaphor: is it ethical? In America, I believe, one could sue for libel, but in Britain one has to shut up and lie low.

What is behind this sad state of affairs? Personally, but I have no way of knowing, I imagine the Prince regrets his few overstatements and in particular his charge of 'inhumanity', because they don't fit with his calls for tolerance and pluralism. Someone – his wife or advisor or editor – might try to stand up to his strong opinions and tell him when he's gone over the top.

The Christian Crusade

But there's a reason these outbursts remain in spite of advice to the contrary. The Prince is conducting a 'crusade', as he calls it, and as in all Holy Wars the 'enemy' is not going to get off lightly. Do I exaggerate? In his speeches over the years he has often alluded to an ideal pre-industrial London dominated by church spires and the dome of St Paul's, a Christian London which he believes has been destroyed by Modernist towers. The accuracy of his analysis may be improved by substituting '19th-century modernisation' for a 20th-century architectural movement, but in some ways his indictment is true. Modernisation, and the ideology and styles of Modernism, have largely been destructive of Christian culture when they haven't been outright agnostic or athiest. As a Christian believer he obviously has an ethical right to damn Modernists, even if he shouldn't call them 'inhuman'. After all, it is humanism they espouse.

At any rate, his advocacy of a Christian culture has become increasingly explicit and, whatever one may think of it, you have to admit it takes incredible courage to promote it on TV to a largely secular nation. In Britain, perhaps more than elsewhere, it is a minor sin to appear too earnest and a major sin to appear foolish, and the Prince risked both when he confronted the nation directly with its lack of faith.

There are several times during the BBC film, especially when he strolls around his house at Highgrove, that he sets a Christian world versus a Modernist wasteland, and his opposition might be most fairly presented through extensive quotation. What you'll miss in my quotes is his sometimes pained and hesitant expression, a clear indication of how difficult it is to speak of such matters to non-believers. He walks towards the camera, sits at a table and says:

> I do like architecture which respects nature. I find it hard, I must say, to appreciate architecture which shouts at you that it is in competition with nature, that it is emphasising the rational element in our humanity to the exclusion of the intuitive. Hence the strictly utilitarian designs: flat roofs, uncompromising angles and absence of decoration . . .

He then goes on to advocate a more organic approach as the camera pans around the vines of his house:

> The trick, it seems to me, is to find ways of enhancing the natural environment, of adding to the sum of human delight by appreciating that man is more, much more than a mere mechanical object whose sole aim is to produce money. Man is a far more complex creation. Above all he has a soul and the soul is irrational, unfathomable, mysterious.
>
> Ever since man began to build, he has acknowledged this vital aspect of himself, whether it be through some form of pagan worship which led him to want to decorate and embellish his buildings, or through a desire to glorify God and to build in sympathy with God's creation on this earth . . .
> Our age is the first to have seen fit to abandon the past or actually to deny its relevance and the lessons learnt over thousands of years. It is the first to have despised the principles of mathematical harmony and proportion and to have embarked on a course which glorifies man's domination over nature and the triumph of science.
> All this coincides with what can only be described as the denial of God's place in the scheme of things and the substitution of man's infallibility. The result, I would suggest, has been a profound dis-ease amongst countless people who are forced to live in the surroundings sired by this unbalanced attitude.

After this point in the film the Prince changes mood and subject as he advocates a variety of architecture that is traditional, decorative, well-scaled and in one case, even, Modern: the addition to Lord's Cricket Ground by Michael Hopkins. He also defends a few Post-Modern buildings and comes close to advocating a thorough-going pluralism, but on the whole his message is a return to tradition and a Christian past. Yet it is one that is to be updated. Using the example of Seaside, the small new village in Florida, and the ideas of its architects and Leon Krier, the Prince puts forward his idea of a new 'Ten Commandments' – 'sensible and widely agreed rules, saying what people can and what they cannot do'. He shows Seaside with its sensible, if modest, neo-Classical rules concerning style and layout, and then says he has asked Leon Krier to design one part of a village, which he owns, with analogous rules. The idea is that within such limits of a Code 'anyone can design their own house' and it will still add to the harmony of the whole.

The Prince ends his film with a look at medieval Sienna where a comparable Code has been operative since 1295, at least in the centre of the city. And he draws from this the lesson connecting traditional planning with Christian society:

> Of course, Sienna was the result of more than just enlightened planning legislation. The city was born of a time when people believed that 'Unless the Lord build the house, they labour in vain that build it'. 'The city is the image of the soul' wrote St Catherine of Sienna . . . The Campo was designed, so it is said, to suggest the protective cloak of the Virgin, lying spread across the heart of the city.
> Those were the days. In our time it's a lucky city, especially in Britain, that doesn't have its heart torn out and thrown away. But it is *our* time. We *can* see reason again if we really want to.

The final words of the Prince, spoken on the royal train to the suitable accompaniment of William Boyce's music, are that we can 'with God's help and inspiration' have beautiful and civilised cities and places.

The Prince's performance, even sermon, was startling by television standards and I don't know of any comparable use of the media in our time. He looked straight into the camera, and six million viewers' eyes, and told them what was wrong with them and what they should do about it. Television is a hot medium, even if McLuhan called it cold, because it grabs the viewer intimately, with all the senses, and allows the presenter to talk in a very personal way. The Prince used TV with maximum effect, radiating the kind of personal warmth and confidentiality that politicians have come to use, and he also showed an understanding of Margaret Thatcher's 'politics of conviction' – the way sharp opinions presented with force can tribalise a nation.

It is this skill which he has used to create what I've called 'new wave monarchy', the new role that royalty is forging, along with the media, to get their views across to a wide audience. This may reach 200 million viewers in the rare case of a royal wedding, but usually it is confined to a national audience and backed up with saturation coverage by the newspapers. The views expressed, as I'm sure you know, are usually apolitical and cover such things as ecology, the ozone layer and pollution, but every now and then the Prince takes a strong stand on inner city renewal and more contentious issues. I mention this wider background because it is essential for understanding the more limited area of the Prince's intervention in the architectural debate. He is using architecture, I believe, as a springboard, or test, for a much larger 'crusade' – the re-establishment of a Christian culture.

The extraordinary aspect of his TV sermon is not just that he had the courage to make it, but that no newspaper or religious leader took up its message. Given the explicitness and reiteration of his call to arms one would have thought some bishop or cleric might have given a national response. But as far as I know the theologians were silent: only his architectural attack hit the headlines. This silence speaks rather loudly, I think, about the secular nature of Britain and the West today and it shows just how difficult it will be for the Prince to win his 'crusade'. We might characterise it as the four C's: Conservation, Community Architecture, Classicism all under the umbrella of Christianity.

This is perhaps a simplification of the Prince's message, but not too far off the mark. It is, if you like, a kind of fundamentalism – explicitly at the architectural level and implicitly as the religious level. It raises all sorts of interesting questions, but I can only comment here on the ethical implications for architecture. The Prince has a perfect right to advocate a view of life and style of architecture in which he believes and a partial right to use his privileged position and media power to his advantage. He obviously has the right, and probably duty, to commission the best Classicists around, such as Leon Krier, to carry out his ideals. But with these rights go certain ethical responsibilities which touch on our sense of fair play. This notion which is ingrained in Britain, it is not too far-fetched to say, through sport, carries the obligation of competition, of an *equal* match between balanced adversaries.

Different ends – fair means

And here we come to murky territory. It is not fair to intervene from a privileged position in public inquiries while the inspector is writing his report; it is not fair to damn architects in such a way that their practice collapses and they have to leave the country (as Stirling has now contemplated). It may be legal, but it doesn't appeal to our sense of a match between equal contestants. It is unfair, un-Christian and distasteful to refer to Modernists as 'inhuman'. It is unfair to use inappropriate similes, such as 'an old wireless', although this brings up matters of judgement (as an architectural critic I find it mistaken). It is unfair of the BBC to mismatch the Prince in a time slot and with an audience of about five times that of Richard Rogers.

Well, I can hear you think, 'whoever said that life is fair, or that Princes are equal to commoners?' No one. But if we have a feeling for ethics and a belief in democracy, as the Prince professes, then as in any adversarial contest in sport or politics, we have an obligation to make the opposing sides much more equal than they are at present.

We are, of course, not just playing a game here, but debating what cities and nature are to be like in ten years time and although many people, including myself, might find much to recommend in the Prince's specific views, we might not share his ultimate goals. And even if we did believe in his four C's, these ends would not justify his unfair means of debate. The problem of living in a pluralist society, where there are different views of the good life, is that individuals and groups will be constantly tempted to impose their views through a momentary privileged position, often as they appeal to democracy. Architects have done this and been rightly accused by the Prince of 'arrogance', an arrogance he has inadvertently followed in setting himself up as an expert on 'ordinary people'. It seems to me the most ethical course to follow in this situation, where 'conviction politics' so dominates the media and many people are looking for the New Ten Commandments (or even fewer) is to insist, more strongly, that those affected by an architect, or Prince are given some real choices, a meaningful vote and a way to get the local environment they want. It's time to call the professed democrats' bluff and demand the real thing.

NEW LIBRARY IN BIRMINGHAM WHICH 'SNUBS' SURROUNDING VICTORIAN BUILDINGS

HRH THE PRINCE OF WALES
Recent Speeches

THE TATE OF THE NORTH

This speech was made at the opening of the new Tate Gallery of the North on 24 April 1988, housed in part of the Grade I listed Albert Dock in Liverpool renovated by James Stirling – an architect who the Prince had previously criticised for his design for No 1 Poultry in London. Prince Charles' commendation of the scheme reflects his interests in conservation and in the value of finding new uses for great industrial buildings of the past in the revitalisation of inner cities.

Ladies and Gentlemen, it does give me particular pleasure to be here today, partly because I came up here, I think it was two years ago, and saw something of the work that was taking place here in the Albert Dock, and having seen it then I got extremely excited by all the possibilities and the various development proposals which were then in the offing, and I thought one of the most imaginative ventures of all was to open a Tate Gallery of the North . . . What is so encouraging, I think, is to see a use for these great buildings having been developed so elegantly and with such enormous skill by a very large team of people who obviously have worked extremely hard. These particular buildings, I think, must have been dramatic to say the least in the 19th century when Prince Albert came up and opened it. Of course in those days it was all full of incredible activity and an immense number of ships. In fact when Queen Victoria came here in 1851, she recorded in her journal – apart from the fact that it was a horrible foggy day and she could hardly see anything (the days before proper anti-pollution measures) – that the whole place was a forest of masts, and obviously it made a great impression on her and Prince Albert at the time.

In those days, these docks were known apparently for their smells apart from anything else, particularly the very good ones – molasses and sugar and hops and malt and things like that – and apparently when the wind was in the right direction people in Liverpool knew exactly where their money would be coming from. Of course Sir Henry Tate, who has been so much involved in this part of the world and in the Tate Gallery originally, made his money from sugar and from inventing the sugar cube. And he, which I think is such a telling fact, put a great deal of the money that he made out of sugar back into the arts and into learning, thus furnishing mankind – as Swift said of the bee – with the two noblest of things, which are sweetness and light! . . .

But I need hardly tell you that I wouldn't really be here unless I felt that this was a particularly encouraging idea, as I said, to bring the Tate collection or part of it up here. One of the things that I feel, having a little bit of Scottish blood in my veins, is it is rather a waste to see parts of these great collections that our museums and galleries have, lingering either in basements or warehouses and very often with not enough resources to maintain them in the condition which they ought to be in. And so this sort of development is of immense importance.

Not only that, but I also feel that by bringing such a collection to the North it is showing how important this part of the world is. Sometimes, I think, people in the South feel that because everything tends to happen in London nobody can be interested in art or culture in the North – and it couldn't be less true. There is an enormous amount of interest and enthusiasm in many parts of the country for exactly this kind of thing, not only in terms of art galleries and museums, but also in terms of theatre, music and opera. I very much hope that this particular development will act as an enormous spur and encouragement to others in other parts of the country, where there are some really wonderful towns and cities with intriguing and marvellous architecture now lying idle and redundant which can be brought back into use again and provide enormous encouragement and pleasure for people in these areas . . .

I do very much hope that because this Tate Gallery of the North has provided a great cultural focus now for Liverpool, that the same thing will happen in other towns and provide that very important element of regeneration and restoration, particularly of confidence of people living in areas that once knew great success and prosperity and which in due course will, I know, return to that eventually.

ROSEHAUGH SELF-BUILD

From criticising the destructive nature of much Modern architecture and urban development, Prince Charles has become increasingly interested in schemes for community participation. In this speech made on 15 September 1988 at the inauguration of the Rosehaugh Self-Build Housing Initiative at Dunbridge Street in the East End of London, he stresses the importance of support from local authorities, building societies and developers such as Godfrey Bradman of Rosehaugh, and the positive effects such a self-build project can bring to both the individual and the community.

Mr Bradman, Ladies and Gentlemen . . . I did want to say how particularly exciting it is for me to be here today, on a rather special occasion as far as I am concerned, as a result of the meeting that I had with Godfrey Bradman and several other people who I invited to lunch at Kensington Palace, I think it must have been two years ago now, to look into this sort of question. And much to my absolute amazement as a result of that lunch and a very interesting discussion that developed, Godfrey Bradman went away with some others, particularly with those from the Borough of Tower Hamlets, and thrashed out a workable scheme which you now see about to develop.

I personally found it extremely encouraging that such an initiative was in the end possible because, as you can imagine, the difficulties and the potential obstacles were immense, and when you also consider that a large number of government departments were involved, a large number of others from different sectors were involved, it has been a great example, I think, of many people working together to produce a highly sensible scheme in the end . . .

This initiative . . . does make sense I think. Apart from anything else, as a result, people can have recognisably proper homes at the end of the day which they have played a full part in actually creating, instead of being part of a vast anonymous labyrinth, which for some people is what happens. And it was most enjoyable, I thought, talking to all those highly courageous and determined people who are building their own homes here, to listen to what they had to say and to hear just how enthusiastic they were in getting to grips with their own houses, many of whom already have skills of bricklaying or plumbing or electrical installation.

All I know, is that if I tried to do it, it would end in total disaster, having already laid one brick in a rather haphazard fashion, so I take my hat off to people who are prepared to build their own houses. Then the actual excitement and involvement of building with your own hands ultimately will mean, I hope, that useful skills are acquired in that process, so that having built your own house and having learnt through making your own mistakes, but also having somebody around to give you helpful advice at the same time, perhaps many people as a result will be able to find jobs in other areas as a result of that experience. This has happened in other projects of this kind in different parts of the country, I know.

Being able to have proper houses in a traditional layout means in the end that you perhaps have a greater sense of community: with things on a more human scale, where children can play in comparative safety, rather than the difficulty which I know many parents have when living in some of the higher blocks of flats. Children can also learn, by having their own recognisable area and garden, to respect other people's property more easily, which again contributes greatly towards that sense of community.

It also enables people to leave something behind which they have created. Ruskin, I think it was, urged that when we build, let us think that we build for ever, and to a certain extent I am sure that the houses that are built here will be houses that should last. I hope that this initiative will provide the kind of housing that is needed in many areas; that it will also help to produce a rather more mixed community which is more economically self-sustaining. Most important of all, is the fact that people should be able to have the sort of home that they want, rather than what others think they should have . . .

Ladies and Gentlemen, it is extremely encouraging as far as I am concerned to see so many public landowners here today, gathered in this creaking tent – which is about to collapse on our heads, I think – because that shows just how interested all of you are . . . I hope that you will see possibilities of this kind of scheme with relevance to your own particular part of the world. I know that the Borough Council of Tower Hamlets has been a most crucial element of this whole initiative in making the land available in the first place. That is obviously extremely important from the point of view of whether this scheme will be seen to have real relevance to inner urban areas where there remain areas of dereliction in public authority and nationalised industry ownership, parts of which perhaps could be utilised for such self-build projects.

Now none of this would have been possible here today without the Halifax Building Society's wonderful involvement. The fact that they are prepared to put quite as much money as they are prepared to do into this will make the whole difference. They have already been extremely helpful in Halifax itself, where Business in the Community has established a one-time partnership scheme, and their involvement there has been absolutely crucial in the development of that partnership and will continue to be so, I know . . .

And I look forward in, I hope perhaps a year's time, to coming back and seeing the end result of the building operations and to see all these people sitting I hope in warm sunshine on their patios outside. I hope they have great success.

ACCESSIBLE HOUSING

In this speech delivered at the Nationwide Anglia/NHBC Design Awards Presentation Ceremony, held on 1 February 1989 at The Grosvenor House, Prince Charles calls for architects and builders to be aware of the special needs of disabled people in designing safe and accessible housing.

. . . Several years have passed since with my Advisory Group on Disability I began discussing with the private house building industry ways to meet the changing needs of users throughout their lives. House buyers' expectations I think have grown somewhat; central heating is now a matter of course, all houses have a fully fitted kitchen and easy access to the garden is generally expected. But the need is for more I think than just this; we are after a secure environment where people can feel safe and yet retain their privacy and houses which everyone can at least visit without having to plan in advance how they can get past the front door; and so the Nationwide Anglia/NHBC Award was established with a challenge of two conflicting features. Security or how to keep unwelcome visitors out, and accessibility or how to clear the way for those who are welcome . . .

It is, I think, particularly fitting that the NHBC should be one of the guiding lights in this particular venture. Their prime task is to try and set standards and to protect buyers of new homes. They were the first to understand our objectives and without the enthusiasm of their management this award could certainly not have been established. I am also greatly heartened to see a leading building society involved in what goes into a home as well as how it is actually financed. The Nationwide Anglia deserves enormous praise for its continuing commitment to these awards. Building societies have recently been thrust further into the maelstrom of commercial life. They face increased competition on all sides and yet this has not prevented them showing an active interest in inner-city developments and housing schemes for the less well off. They have made clear that they have a true commitment to helping improve the way people live. The friendly society heritage and traditions do still flourish I would suggest.

Now the categories of the award are important, obviously it is necessary to gain the allegiance of the trend setters, the volume house builders, if these criteria are to be broadly accepted. But the personal attention the smaller builder gives to his customers' needs are equally important. His interest and understanding is something which the larger building firms might perhaps do well to adopt. Most encouraging is the example set by the written charter of one major national company, *Ideal Homes*, a schedule of standards which all their managers must observe.

Now Ladies and Gentlemen, I recognise that the criteria for these awards have presented builders with something of a technical challenge, particularly in relation to the height of the threshold and the approach paths. Yet I suspect these standards can be met and the results still be aesthetically pleasing. Different ground levels between houses could be dealt with perhaps, by imaginative landscaping, by a path being brought in from a different angle or by using shrubs to give visual interest rather than creating barriers with steps. Barretts have shown, for instance, that you can at least combine steps with a ramp at the side which offers a useful compromise . . . Awkward thresholds and flights of steps cause irritation and stress to the elderly (and those of us over 40 are beginning to find that out) and to parents of young children as well as those in wheelchairs. Increasingly, elderly people wish to retain their independence in their own homes and often it is the lack of a downstairs lavatory, for instance, that forces them into moving.

The recent Office of Population Censuses and Surveys reports on disability among adults, highlighted clearly the need to ensure that the disabled people's needs are to be fully taken into account when planning new housing. There are some 6.2 million people in Great Britain with some form of disability or other. Of those, only 400,000 or 7 per cent were in a communal establishment. So this leaves over 5.8 million people with some form of disability who must cope with living in housing which can be extremely inadequate for their own particular disability.

Good homes begin on the drawing board. Good homes are built because rigorous standards are laid down and adhered to by all within the industry. But it is not the financial constraints which create barriers in housing but lack of awareness, so it might help possibly if every architect and builder were to try life in a wheelchair for a short time or perhaps a few designers ought to spend a day confined in one and then they could perhaps experience some of the difficulties facing those with disabilities. Like switches out of reach, doors too narrow and heavy to open, taps that are difficult or impossible to run and the many other things that can cause rage and frustration to the wheelchair user. But from the point of view of the individual affected it is the house that may have the disability sometimes and not the person.

It would be nice to think that planners and builders might set aside a little time occasionally to understand the needs of all the house buyers and appreciate that these needs do not always remain static. All of us at some time of our lives may well have a temporary disability ranging from backache, which seems to be one of the major problems which affects most of us, or a broken ankle, to the permanency of paralysis from a stroke or a road accident.

As the number of the elderly in our society grows, more homes combining the ideals of security and accessibility will be needed. Though some may choose to do so for a variety of reasons, it is, I think, only sensible to ask whether people should have to leave their homes simply because of the onset of age or infirmity.

So, Ladies and Gentlemen, I hope that these awards will become stronger with each year that passes and influence more professionals within the industry to take accessibility, security and safety a little bit more into account. They could become a cornerstone for a set of standards that will have a beneficial long-term effect on the way we live and that will ensure that awareness of the needs of wheelchair users becomes as natural for house designers and estate planners as ensuring that the plumbing actually works.

BUILD A BETTER BRITAIN

At the opening of the Build a Better Britain *exhibition at the Business Design Centre, Islington, London, on April 1989, Prince Charles as Patron of the Civic Trust makes a plea for local identity and pride in construction, as against the anonymity of estates that could be anywhere. He then changes theme to express his deep concern at an issue recently brought to the attention of the West, the so-called 'systemisation' programme of President Ceausescu of Romania by which thousands of villages and communities, and with them a whole cultural heritage, are being destroyed to be replaced by the tower blocks of urban collectives.*

Ladies and Gentlemen, I must confess that I had somehow imagined that I was coming to a rather small and intimate gathering, but I have been rather mistaken and have discovered that it is much larger than I thought, and nor was I expecting quite so many eminent property developers and architects and builders. But it is very encouraging to see so many of you, and to have had a chance to see a few anyway of the exhibits. There is never enough time on these occasions but at least I have had a glimpse. I am also very impressed, if I may say so, by the restoration work and the conversion work that has gone on in this building. I think that it really is very impressive indeed. I am not too sure about the acoustics, but still . . .

The Civic Trust itself has of course been promoting quality in the built environment for many years and in a variety of ways. Two years ago at the first exhibition, the Trust unveiled a new Regeneration Unit, whose purpose is to restore life to communities laid waste by economic and social change. It had the aim of building on the Trust's experience, particularly in Wirksworth and Halifax. Any of you who have seen what has been achieved in those two very different places – and I was in Wirksworth earlier this week in the snow – will know as I do that a community-based approach, sensitive to the environment, can have remarkable results, physically and economically.

The Unit is now working in nearly 20 locations in England and bidding soon to extend into Wales and Northern Ireland. I am particularly pleased to say that there is to be a Trust follow-up to their original initiative with a call to action by others in the form of a Regeneration Campaign . . . The campaign will be launched formally in September, but I can say now that the aim is to set up more than 100 projects over the next five years. BiC [Business in the Community] and Groundwork are working with the Civic Trust to put the campaign together, but I do hope it will draw in bodies of all kinds because the need for it is evident.

If we were dropped blindfolded into the heart of any British village and had the blindfold removed, would you know where you were? Once not long ago you could have recognised the region from the distinctive local materials. The beauty and variety of those materials is breathtaking – flint in Norfolk, timber in Kent, limestone in Northumberland, cob and thatch in Devon and so on *ad infinitum*. This is part of our architectural inheritance. 'And we', as William Morris said, 'are its trustees for those who come after us.' Compton Martin, Castle Rising, Kilpeck, Ryme Intrinsica, Winterborne Bassett and Widecombe-in-the-Moor conjure up an archetypal picture of village life. The buildings they constructed then were built well and built to last. The stone masons, the bricklayers and the carpenters were building for their sons and their successive generations. They were building with purpose and love and, above all, with pride.

So if we are to build a better Britain – if we are to leave anything of lasting beauty for our children to be proud of – we must search out that quality which our forebears knew so well. There are builders all over the country who know about that quality, especially family firms where skills have been passed from father to son. There are bricklayers, carpenters, plasterers who are every bit as skilful as those of past generations, but who are seldom asked to deviate from the norm. The norm is what we see in ever-increasing numbers on the edges of our precious villages, or squashed like bad sets of irregular teeth between the cottage and the school.

If we are to build a better Britain, which so many people seem to want, then we need to seek inspiration from the intuitive ability of our forbears to build in harmony with their surroundings and to express the essence of their humanity through the design and layout of their dwellings and public buildings, thereby creating a true sense of community and, above all, of belonging.

We all know the type of developer who has no real interest in the lives of our villages or towns, except for the profit they might engender; he was not born in Snettisham or Gittisham or Slad. He probably buys up the land at the back of the school playground and next to the 1930s council houses. He then applies for planning permission for 25 houses. He does not notice the gentle curve and winding of the street which follows the contour of the land, but sets his houses down in all directions.

The village is then up in arms, planning permission turned down. Such is the system that this makes little difference. He will appeal and re-appeal because he can afford to. Eventually, the houses will come. The designers of them will doubtless make a gesture towards the local styles and materials in order to appease the conservationists – what more do they want, once they've got their pantiles and Georgian fanlights? But the details are *just* wrong; the eaves are too mean or the building manual which was consulted has come up with windows of the wrong proportions and, where are the chimneys? Is nobody ever going to burn a fire again? Perhaps.

These important considerations may not concern the developer and, anyway, he has doubtless already moved on and is appealing on another site. Now this new estate could be anywhere in England, for the materials used are universal. But let us not be too gloomy, we have got it in us to build well, as I've seen in several places all over Britain. We must demand nothing less than this high standard if our future villages and towns are to remain as beautiful and as socially cohesive as many of them still are.

I need hardly say that there are many lessons from which we, and others, can learn. We in this country are painfully aware of the trauma caused by uprooting traditional communities at the behest of 'benevolent', know-all planners. We hope that we have learnt something from such an experience. That process should have made us, therefore, all the more sensitive to the awful spectre of an entire society, not just certain districts, losing its roots and its ancient communities, which is what is happening today in a corner of Eastern Europe, in a country called Romania. There, President Ceaucescu has embarked on the wholesale destruction of his country's cultural and human heritage.

What happened here in the 1960s is, of course, not comparable with the policy known as 'systematisation' which aims to transform Romania's rural environment into over 500 urban collectives designated as 'agro-industrial complexes'. The object, which is very interesting, is to reshape the nation's identity, to create a new type of person utterly subordinate to its dreams. To achieve this, President Ceaucescu has set about destroying the cities and villages of his country and replacing them with blocks of flats which are a repetition of failed 1960s social engineering, mixed with the atmosphere of George Orwell's *1984*. (Let me emphasise here, for the benefit of those who specialise in making headlines from the most unlikely sources, that I am not comparing Romania in some way with Great Britain.) To achieve this plan, some 8,000 villages could be demolished, together with churches, ancestral graveyards and every connection with the rural people's past.

In this regard, I am aware of, and support, the moves made both by the British Government and its European partners to bring pressure to bear on the Romanian Government to reverse its policies. The 20th century has witnessed some strange aberrations of the human spirit, but few can match the activities of rulers who boast about their patriotism and then systematically undertake the destruction of the cultural heritage of their people. The extraordinary cultural diversity of Romania is not only part of her natural wealth but a possession of inestimable value to all of humanity.

It is difficult, I find, to remain silent as the peasant traditions and ancient buildings of a fellow European society are bulldozed to make way for a uniform and deathly mock-modernity. Believe it or not, I have a small personal share in this unfolding tragedy because the tomb of my great great great grandmother – Claudina, Countess Rhedey, who was my great grandmother, Queen Mary's grandmother, and Hungarian – is in the village of Singiorge de Padure and threatened with demolition.

Imagine the horror of your entire ancestral community being levelled in front of your eyes – including buildings dating from the Middle Ages – or of the centres of ancient towns with their monuments, churches, monasteries swept away regardless of

architectural merit, religious significance or symbolic importance to the Romanian people. The appalling human tragedy has been eloquently expressed in an open letter to the Romanian President which was published in this country. It is worth listening to because, apart from anything else, it sums up what should lie at the very heart of our aim to build a better Britain and, above all, to build communities with a soul. This is what the letter says:

> We call on you to stop the demolition of the country's villages. Driving people from their ancestral settlements where they have a purpose, where they have houses built to meet the needs of life and labour, is a sacrilege. The peasant house is identified with the soul of its builder. By striking at the peasant house, by replacing it with a pokey flat in a tower-block, you strike not only at the soul of the people but also at the patrimony which belongs to all mankind.

Ladies and gentlemen, clearly what they need in Romania is a Civic Trust! It gives me great pleasure to declare this exhibition open.

COMMUNITY ENTERPRISE AWARDS

In this speech at the presentation of The Times/RIBA Community Enterprise Awards for 1988-89, at the RIBA on 27 June 1989, Prince Charles talks about his experience of the communication problems in convincing a sceptical public and business world of the success and viability of community projects. He stresses the importance of the process of participation often as much as the end result – here we are not looking at 'great Architecture' or for perfection but at the human benefits from such award-winning schemes as CARE, a project to help people take responsibility for their own environment in West Barnsley, and Antur Waufawr a building and community workforce project bringing together the able-bodied and mentally handicapped in a village in North Wales – and the need in all schemes, whether inner-city renewal or the proposed Dorchester development, to take the long-term view.

It has been remarkable, I think, to see how the awareness of community architecture and what community enterprise can achieve, to see how it has been growing gradually over the last few years. Very often these things take so much longer to put across than people would ever imagine and patience and determination are obviously needed. I find my problem so often in these areas where one's trying to persuade people that in fact there are alternative ways of doing things, or ways of doing things which can add to the existing methods of approaching problems, the trouble is that I frequently hear myself repeating constantly the message and in the end I get bored of it. One forgets that other people haven't always heard it and the difficulty is, you know, how actually to communicate ideas or ways of doing things to people, because so often many more people than you think don't actually know what is possible, or what is happening, or what the best practices are.

I believe very strongly myself in disseminating if you can, as widely as possible, best practices. But the only way to do that, I've learnt, is actually to take people to see what the best projects are. You can't I've discovered necessarily persuade people or convert them by showering them with leaflets or pamphlets or even speeches or videos or whatever, but if people can actually see for themselves and talk to the relevant people who've been through whatever process it is or whatever experience it is, then so often people begin to realise what the possibilities are and this, I think, is the crucial factor in all these exercises of community enterprise. So many people are sceptical about it until they actually see it and I bet a lot of you here were pretty sceptical until you actually got involved yourselves.

I know that from the point of view of scepticism it is obviously a difficulty and I know that some developers and others see a useful marketing arm nowadays in utilising community architecture for perhaps some publicity purposes, but in some cases of course this merely camouflages an otherwise ordinary speculative scheme. For many people the time-scale involved in a community architecture approach or in a community enterprise approach often seems too laborious or too inefficient and rather time wasting when time and money are always at a premium. So the difficulty, it seems to me, is how to ensure that the long-term considerations are taken into account rather than just the short-term, which tend to be, I think, the norm. But as the President of the RIBA was saying just now, the *process* of the community architecture approach is as important as the actual product and it is so often the process which leads to greater things in the future.

So as I say, it is important, I think, from the point of view of development of the kind of community enterprise you represent that people see in order to believe. I have found the same thing was true with a venture that we undertook in the Duchy of Cornwall in Kennington with a large block of flats built in the 1930s called Newquay House . . . When I suggested that we look at an alternative means of maintaining the property and ensuring that the tenants had a say in the running of it and in the design of the renovation and everything else, when we initially suggested this there was a great deal of scepticism I think amongst the tenants themselves until they went to see another project elsewhere in the country. And then having talked to others who had been through the same process, they came back with the light of conversion in their eye. Since then it has taken a lot of patience and a lot of frustration, but now the project is off the ground and under way and I hope will provide the kind of result that people want.

You can never have an ideal solution, that I totally understand, and we should never expect there to be an ideal solution, but at least it is an attempt to arrive at a more satisfactory arrangement. I have also been terribly impressed with what I've seen of the Eldonians project up in Liverpool, which I went to help inaugurate with Tony McGann earlier this year and that again is seeing in order to believe. My problem is I see all these things and I can't understand why other people can't always see the way in which community involvement and energy and enthusiasm can be released by such people as Tony McGann and so many others who are in this room now, but they will, in the end, get the message I am sure.

But what to me seems to be the crucial factor in all this is leadership – this whole question of identifying real force of personality; those people who have the talent and the abilities and the intelligence and the determination to help lead others and to show others the way and set them an example of how actually you can do a considerable amount for yourselves and with yourselves rather than waiting for somebody else to come and do it for you and this, to my mind, is one of the most important areas of all. For instance, with the recent Housing Action Trust Reports prepared by private consultants for the Department of the Environment, these Reports show that using traditional methods, for instance bringing builders in to repair property and bringing the property up to standard, will involve very high costs indeed and whilst some of these Reports recommend residents participation, I don't think you can over-emphasise the need to tap the potential talent of ordinary people in these particular areas where the problems are greatest.

What is lacking, it seems to me, is proper leadership training for such people to help them to understand the basic principles, for instance of development, finance, marketing and so on. In Business in the Community, of which I am President, we are now trying to examine how to achieve just this kind of training as a sort of pilot project, because otherwise there is simply not the money nor the personnel available to carry out the task on what has now become the conventional basis. The hidden resources of ordinary people out there, yourselves, need to be one of the main driving forces in regeneration assisted obviously, by professional enablers who understand how to make a practical reality of the residents desire for a true neighbourhood – a true neighbourhood feeling, the atmosphere that can be engendered by such a community. Obviously you need the kind of professionals who have the patience and the tolerance and the understanding to enable this sort of thing to happen. It is not easy, by any means, and it also seems to me that one of the great difficulties is to get the community representatives themselves to agree. So often, if you are not careful, people end up in little factions and the problem is compounded. This I think is another area which obviously is absolutely vital.

. . . I have conducted my own experiment in consultation and participation in Dorchester recently when John Thompson attempted the impossible and spent four days over a weekend, consulting the local people in Dorchester and involving them as much as possible, those who were interested, in proposals for further development on the edge of Dorchester . . . And there, it seemed to me, that boldness and above all a long-term vision was called for.

Of course the development on the outskirts of a country town is something rather different from the point of view of how you embark on this from an inner-urban area. But some of the principles obviously are the same and the planning weekend that we had involved very much an act of faith, I believe, but it did generate public enthusiasm and debate which, of course, was the essence of the exercise. It brought out lots of ideas which otherwise would not have been brought out . . . It also produced, obviously, problems and complaints and misunderstandings. Obviously it would be much easier not to build all over green fields but clearly there are requirements for such things as starter homes and for homes for people on lower incomes, so it is essential, it seems to me, to consider the whole exercise on a long-term basis.

We also discovered you can't please everybody and that you all know about. But the aim, as far as we are concerned, is to enable the local community to be and to continue to be involved in the future of their town, with local architects as much as possible, local builders, calling on local skills, again as far as is possible, and also with self-building skills being harnessed at the same time. So it seems to me that the secret, somehow, is to find a way whereby those involved in development can take the long-term view beyond immediate profit and that those who live in communities need to take a wider view, in other words beyond their own immediate interests, to the interests of the organic whole of which they form a part.

As I say, Ladies and Gentlemen, I have been enormously impressed by the schemes that I have seen, by the various projects which are now under way in various parts of London and elsewhere and I know that these projects very often met with immense obstacles and barriers and frustrations, but many of you are still pioneering in this area and we all depend on your determination and enthusiasm and, what's more as I feel very strongly, that you need to write up your experiences or find somebody who can, so that your experience and the knowledge of what mistakes you may have made on the path can be learnt by others.

SCOTTISH NATIONAL PARKS

The Prince's concern for conservation and the environment is revealed in this speech, delivered on 4 July 1989 at the Scottish conference on National Parks, organised by the Countryside Commission for Scotland, in which he argues for more sensitive management and planning, encouraging a greater public understanding of environmental issues.

Mr Chairman, Ladies and Gentlemen, . . . it seems to me that everyone who loves Scotland for its unique and invaluable qualities is agreed upon *one* thing; that somehow a way has to be found to conserve the wild places and the wildlife that inhabits them, as a Scottish resource to be passed on as intact and unimpaired as possible to future generations. It is the very long-term conservation of this unique and delicate habitat in the face of the many conflicting and potentially destructive short-term interests, that presents the real challenge . . .

I know that most of you spend your lives trying to strike a balance in these desperately difficult and highly emotive debates. That is why it is so important that there should be the widest possible consultation before any decisions are ultimately taken. I believe that the key element in meeting this challenge is good management, based on balanced countryside planning. This will have to recognise that different areas have different needs and problems. There will be a need to win the confidence of local communities and landowners, to respect traditional patterns of land use, and for an awareness that in some areas the local economy is as fragile and in need of protection as the environment. The question of public access will be crucial. The urge for recreation is obviously a good thing. On the other hand, we can already see clearly that uncontrolled mass use of certain areas can inflict unacceptable environmental damage, disrupt local communities and cause conflict with other landusers . . . Sensitive management will become more and more important, but so will sensitive education.

In many areas, tourism plays a major part in sustaining the local economy, and of course there is pressure for increased development to provide more employment . . . But we have so few areas of real wilderness left to us that we must protect those we have with particular vigilance . . . There are other areas, away from the wilderness and closer to the centres of population, where it may be appropriate to have a slightly different approach.

I have so far avoided using the term 'National Park'. That is because I simply do not know whether or not this designation would be right for the particular needs and problems of Scotland. It may be that a close study of some of the existing co-ordinated management systems already in operation may reveal that further development of such systems may be more appropriate . . .

Whatever the case, I shall look forward to hearing what you finally decide on this very complicated matter.

BLACKBURN PARTNERSHIP

This speech, delivered on 6 July 1989 to the Blackburn Partnership, a group formed to confront issues such as urban regeneration and the transformation of derelict areas in Blackburn, continues to reflect the Prince's growing concern with environmental issues and his belief in the important role of businesses in working with the community to realise the potential of the urban environment.

I know that action to improve the environment is being put very high on the agenda, and that there has been a very sudden change in attitudes towards the environment chiefly due, I suspect, to determined consumer pressure . . . It's easy, I think, to become very demoralised by the sheer scale of the problem as an individual . . . but I do believe that businesses can do a great deal to contribute towards environmental improvement . . . obviously a great deal more can be done in partnership with the local community to improve the environment around offices and factories, to clear up derelict sites and create a positive atmosphere. Businesses can assist in many grass-roots Community Groups and voluntary organisations which are working to improve the environment such as Civic Trust, Tidy Britain Group, UK 2000 and Groundwork Foundation, and I know that the Partnership is hoping to set up a Groundwork Trust here in Blackburn . . . I am also very glad to hear that there is a proposal to launch a Prince of Wales Community Venture here in Blackburn and that, I hope, will prove to be as effective as in Sunderland, South Wales and Birmingham where we already have projects going, and I hope that this particular venture might have a special emphasis on the service to improve the environment . . . there are obviously opportunities for sensitively developed tourism and leisure, and there are also definitely opportunities for innovative new businesses in environmental protection and control . . .

. . . if I could just rhetorically ask why I go on about environmental improvement and regeneration, I'll tell you why . . . it's because I've seen the dramatic effects of courageous and far-sighted decisions to invest in environmental improvements in urban areas . . . You don't have to look much further than Glasgow to see again the transformation in attitudes which has been brought about through environmental and cultural initiatives stimulating further investment. Nobody would have believed ten years ago that Glasgow would have been designated the European City for culture in 1990; also you only have to look at Lancaster where I was this morning to see a very remarkable development of the Whitecross Industrial and Commercial complex, which began six years ago when nobody wanted to know. They have transformed an area of otherwise unused mill buildings which were going to be knocked down and turned into rather less appropriate developments, and there they have achieved something quite remarkable, when everyone told them it couldn't be done; they put in £5m of public money and £5m of private and the results have been very spectacular . . .

So there are in Blackburn great opportunities I believe, but somebody as always in these things has to make the first move and that is always the difficulty. One of the great secrets it seems to me is how to restore pride and confidence in a community which has suffered from one setback after another and has witnessed an increasing and insidious spread of dereliction. You have only to look, for instance, at the Canal area, which nobody even bothered to look at until fairly recently; nobody could see the value and potential in what appeared to be just a mess. But now people have realised the potential in the restoration of those buildings that line the Canal and in the local character they represent. People are beginning to see the real possibilities that exist also for the town centre, but please, above all, don't be afraid to seek some inspiration from the past and from the local vernacular of Lancashire. Our ancestors didn't get everything right but they weren't fools . . . We need to remember that in many cases our surroundings need to relate to the human scale and to what makes human beings comfortable and neighbourly. So many Lancashire towns have a great deal of immense potential in this area, so do look again at your own canals and derelict industrial buildings, and don't let them fall down or knock them down without very careful reflection because they are one of your greatest assets . . . Ladies and Gentlemen, keep up the good work in Blackburn – it's very encouraging.

THE GREENING OF ARCHITECTURE
Charles Knevitt

L TO R: JOHN THOMPSON, LEON KRIER & PRINCE CHARLES, POUNDBURY, DORCHESTER

As Correspondent to *The Times* and Secretary of *The Times*/RIBA Community Enterprise Scheme, Charles Knevitt is well known for his writings on Community Architecture, which has found an outspoken and influential adherent in the Prince. Here he discusses its development and critical acceptance as a movement founded on social idealism, defined by its belief in the creative interaction between the architect and community as a whole.

The Heroic Period of Community Architecture is dead – the Greening of Architecture has only just begun. The start of a new decade – the 1990s – will come to be seen as a watershed, I predict, as confidently as one can whilst still in the midst of what has been called the 'quiet revolution'.[1] Mysterious portents signal conflicting and sometimes contradictory paths which the movement might follow as we near the millenium. Meanwhile, activity on the ground – the process by which architecture comes into being, and the product which is the legacy for future generations – will be treated as test beds by historians and sociologists of the 21st century, eager to pronounce on whether the architecture of social responsibility and democratic accountability lived up to its promises.

Community architects and community architecture are not unique to Britain, far from it. In America they talk about citizen or social architecture; in China and Indonesia, barefoot architects help villagers to build their own homes. Christopher Alexander has developed a sophisticated 'pattern language' for the production of homes and carried out experimental projects in places such as Mexicali, Mexico. After the devastating earthquake which left 350,000 homeless in Mexico City, in 1985, it was the damnificados (earthquake victims) who demanded responsibility for the rebuilding programme and achieved spectacular results within a matter of months.

Along the Shimshal Valley of northern Pakistan, where subsistence farmers earn £100 a year, and in the *katchi abadis* squatter settlements of Karachi, where three million of the seven million inhabitants live in illegal hovels, community architecture exists in different guises, providing a stark contrast with famous home-grown schemes such as Black Road, Macclesfield, yet whose similarities of approach and implementation are almost uncanny. Lessons from the urban poor's experience in Third World countries are well documented[2] and case studies there go back almost 40 years. The civil rights movement, urban riots and 'advocacy planning' network of neighbourhood advice centres in low income areas of downtown USA in the 1960s are the immediate precedents to what has happened in Britain over the past 20 years, however.[3]

For in 1969 events conspired to launch the Heroic Period of Community Architecture. The then Ministry of Housing and Local Government published the Skeffington Report, which called for public participation in the planning process. The housing charity, Shelter, launched its Neighbourhood Action Project (SNAP) in Liverpool, with its own resident architect. Interaction and Free Form Arts Trust set up independent environmental aid agencies committed to working with local community organisations. And at Byker, in Newcastle upon Tyne, Ralph Erskine – later to receive the Royal Gold Medal for Architecture – set up a site office in a disused funeral parlour to manage a huge rebuilding of the slum area involving existing residents in design decisions.

It was J M (now Sir James) Richards, of all people, who was among the earliest champions of what became known, in a profile of Rod Hackney, in 1975, as Community Architecture.[4] Richards, editor of the *Architectural Review* and Architecture Correspondent of *The Times*, wrote in 1970 that architects should become the equivalent of the local family doctor, developing an intimate knowledge of his patients:

> Architects should similarly have a long-term relationship with one area for which they should feel wholly responsible and to whom anyone with a building problem in the area should automatically turn because of their involvement in its history . . . Like the family doctor, who knows everyone's history, this local architect should be familiar with every street, every tree, every lamp-post, every sign, every boundary wall . . . Again like the doctor, he should – ideally – live there as well as work there.

An even earlier supporter of the not yet nascent movement was Denys (later Sir Denys) Lasdun, architect of the National Theatre and another Royal Gold Medallist. Writing in *The Times* in 1961, he called for an 'enlarged architectural conscience brought about by the greatly increased participation of more people as partial clients'. This would be a better system than introducing 'the most scrupulously applied aesthetic controls'. Society should be a partner in the creative process, to provide decent surroundings for people 'and to help them to a wider vision of life'. But until the first Royal intervention in 1984, when the Prince of Wales attacked the now infamous 'monstrous carbuncle' and 'giant glass stump' in his Hampton Court speech to architects celebrating the 150th anniversary of the RIBA, Community Architecture stirred little interest outside the profession. And while the media focused their attention on what the Prince chose to criticise, it is usually forgotten that he also told his captive audience about the benefits of the Community Architecture approach, praising two architects by name: Rod Hackney and Ted Cullinan. The former claims to have made a thousand enemmies that night, later prompting him to run successfully for the presidencies of the RIBA and International Union of Architects (UIA); while the latter was surprised and slightly embarrassed to discover that the Prince considered him 'a man after my own heart' for designing buildings that were 'beautiful as well as socially useful'.

Royal endorsement brought with it not only a higher public profile, but the respectability and credibility it had hitherto lacked. But as the Prince was soon to demonstrate, his remarks were not just some idle phrases dreamt up by a script-writer. They were his very own words and he was committed. Over the next few months and years, he visited more than a score of Community Architecture projects throughout the country; hosted private dinners for community architects, educationalists, builders, developers, financiers and government officials at Kensington Palace; became patron of *The Times*/RIBA Community Enterprise Awards scheme; commissioned community architects on his Duchy of Cornwall estate; and gave a succession of equally fiery speeches to businessmen, builders and others concerned with bringing about a 'renaissance' of Britain, not least in its inner cities. When it came to releasing Leon Krier's master plan for Poundbury, outside Dorchester, it was the Prince alone (and against the advice of some of his courtiers) who decided to appoint Hunt Thompson Associates to conduct a planning weekend along Community Architecture principles. Soon afterwards, the master plan was undergoing some significant modifications as a result of feedback from local people who attended the event.

While recent attention has focused on the Prince's interest on what one might describe as the stylistic elements of the architectural equation, with his 'A Vision of Britain' television documentary, the publication of his book and opening of the Victoria and Albert Museum exhibition, his interest and involvement in Community Architecture should not be under-estimated. The immediate reason for taking up the cause might well have been his genuine horror at the unsightliness of what had been built in Britain during the post-war period, and with much justification;

and that surely the response from the profession could be no worse if they had some positive input from the users of their products. Also, that alienation of people from their immediate physical environment was a contributory factor in the spate of urban riots that took place in the early-1980s, a problem which community architects were actively addressing.

But we should also bear in mind that Princes with 10, possibly even 20 years to go before they succeed to the throne, can afford to become involved in longer term issues, such as improving standards of professional service and producing more responsive places in which people want to live. Talking about his role as Prince of Wales and heir apparent, he once said: 'There isn't any power. But there can be influence. The influence is in direct proportion to the respect people have for you'. In the cause of Community Architecture, the influence he exerts is a most effective weapon. Of even greater significance, however, is the fact that he practices what he preaches: community architects such as Joe Poynton, based in St Ives, Cornwall, have worked on his Duchy estate at Curry Mallet, in Somerset; and Hunt Thompson at Newquay House, Kennington, south London, and at Poundbury, Dorchester. The Prince is, therefore, leading by example the scale of projects – and his personal financial growing all the time.

None of this is much comfort, though, to mainstream practitioners in the profession he has persistently ridiculed, upbraided and coerced for more than five years. The Royal Institute of British Modernists, as Charles Jencks likes to call it, has produced few stars that the Prince can stomach: Michael Hopkins, the acceptable face of Hi-Tech; Jeremy Dixon, with his traditional modern vernacular housing; and a handful of others. The Prince's intervention had a more dramatic effect on the institutional politics of 66 Portland Place, with president Michael Manser deeply embarrassed by the Hampton Court affair; Royal Gold Medallist Charles Correa put in the shade while receiving his gong, endorsed by the Queen; Manser's successor, Larry Rolland, engaging in open warfare with Hackney and the Institute's own Community Architecture Group; and the eventual election of Hackney to the presidency in 1986, for a two-year term from 1987, in a record poll.

In retrospect, the zenith of the Heroic Period of Community Architecture can be pinpointed to six days in November/December 1986. The first four were taken up with the 1,000-delegate Building Communities Conference, at the Astoria Theatre, London; on the fifth day we rested; and on the sixth, Hackney's election to the RIBA presidency was announced.

The conference, reported the *Architectural Review* four months later, 'brought together on the same platform representatives of all the main political parties [including the Greens], of building and environmental professions, of business and industry, radical community groups, the established church, and, of course, the monarchy'. Among the speakers were household names such as Lord Scarman, Michael Heseltine, Shirley Williams and Simon Jenkins, while heros of the community development movement such as Paddy Doherty, Tony McGann, George Nicholson, Frances McCall and Ted Watkins were given equal billing. And then there was the Prince of Wales.

Given the theme, the personalities and the launch of what were intended to be two public fund-raising appeals, it was hardly surprising that the event made the front page of every national newspaper, 15 television news and current affairs programmes, 27 national and local radio news and current affairs programmes and thousands of column inches elsewhere. At last there seemed to be some consensus, a common agenda for action. All the interested parties assembled in one place and at one time to thrash out the issues, instead of sniping from the sidelines. What is more, and the significance of this should not be lost, it was architects committed to Community Architecture who made it all happen.[5]

And just days before Hackney took up his RIBA presidency, Margaret Thatcher won her third successive election victory. From the staircase of the Conservative Party's Central Office that very night, she uttered for the first time those magic words: 'inner cities'.

If Building Communities was the zenith, with Hackney's election victory and the inner cities' belated arrival on the political agenda following in its wake, that begs a number of questions about the current state of Community Architecture: what is it now and where is it going; is it truly architecture at all; and what might fill the vacuum created by the end of its Heroic Period? But first we should ask ourselves: what makes the years 1969-89 the Heroic Period in the first place and what led to its demise? Here there are useful comparisons with what Jencks calls the Heroic Period of the idealist tradition in Modern architecture.[6] During the period from about 1920-50, Jencks argues, Le Corbusier, Mies van der Rohe and Walter Gropius were the principal protagonists of 'alternative visions to the existing social order'. Their common social ideals were based on humanitarian liberalism, reformist pluralism and a vague social Utopianism. In *Towards a New Architecture*, published in 1923, Corb stated emphatically: 'It is a question of building which is at the root of the social unrest of today; architecture or revolution'. Three years later, in *The City of Tomorrow*, he added: 'Things are not revolutionised by making revolutions. The real Revolution lies in the solution of existing problems'. As we shall see in a moment, especially with reference to CIAM, the politics of the reforming heros was somewhat confused, at best, or probably apolitical if taken to its logical conclusion. But what became of the movement they were promoting for 30 years, interrupted though it was by World War Two? Jencks states:

> Basically, the social Utopianism which existed in the work of Le Corbusier, Gropius and the CIAM architects became deflected just as their Modern aesthetic – the International Style – triumphed around the world in the 50s. In effect, what was known popularly as 'Modern Architecture' became accepted by most national governments as well as the leading international /. . . /. . . corporations and it was, most importantly, stripped of its social idealism. As a result of this mixed success, Modern architecture became identified with the bureaucracies that commissioned, inhabited and sometimes even designed it. The ambiguities that this could produce were extraordinary, since much of the International Style had previously been associated with progressive social institutions.

Community architects are the successors to the heros of the idealist tradition. They share 'alternative visions to the existing social order'. While some are fired with revolutionary fervour, most are happy to develop very pragmatic responses to what already exists, in a way that Corb advocated. Like the founding members of CIAM, they have common cause yet do not subscribe to one political ideology – anarchist, socialist, pragmatist, even capitalist. This causes inevitable hostility among critics who cannot get to grips with Community Architecture: some claim it is a Marxist conspiracy to transfer 'power to the people'; others that it is one of the main instruments of Thatcherite policies, actively aiding and abetting the annihilation of local government. Worst of all, in the architectural critic's eye, is the fact that its coinage is process not product. There is not an identifiable Community Architecture Style. Therefore, the frustrated critic argues, it cannot be architecture! Before dealing with the architecture in Community Architecture, what has happened to the movement to indicate that its Heroic Period is well and truly over? The central tenet of community architects is

that the users of their work should be actively involved in commissioning, helping to design, even building it on occasions, and then managing it. This is a political decision, taken by architects. In an ideal world, the users should also have the resources (principally land and money) to act as 'developer', because while the built environment is improved by participation in the process; controlling the process is even better.

What has happened over the past three years is that this central tenet has been endorsed by all the major political parties (Liverpool's Militant-controlled council has in the recent past been its only main opponent), by leading churchmen, local authorities and others in positions of power and influence – and not least, of course, by the users themselves and the Prince of Wales. Community Architecture in the 1980s has reached the same position as the International Style in the 1950s. Its success has led to its adoption by the mainstream – government (central and local), the private sector (Business in the Community, backed by 400 of Britain's top companies, is now committed to the Community Architecture approach), and quangos which are a significant force in the marketplace, such as the Housing Corporation which finances housing associations and self-build groups.

We will have to wait and see whether the movement's 'social idealism' remains intact. American experience suggests that perhaps it will not. During the 1970s, 80 community design centres were set up in the US run by idealistic young professionals, who believed that they should 'enable' people to solve their problems, not 'provide' ready-made solutions. They were, in the words of Dr Tony Gibson, of the Town and Country Planning Association, 'on tap', not 'on top'. Community technical aid centres are the British equivalent, but they are struggling in the face of grant cutbacks. As federal budget cutbacks began to bite in America in the Reagan era, so also the centres there became either institutionalised, or marginalised, and the 'social idealism' was lost.

At the same time, the direction, leadership and momentum so desperately needed by the movement and provided by Rod Hackney until his election as RIBA president, disappeared virtually overnight as he took up his post and that of president of the UIA. Consequently, the initiative moved from architects to No 10 Downing Street, corporate boradrooms, council chambers and tenant meetings.

Having gained recognition, acceptability and been absorbed by the mainstream, the future of Community Architecture lies in the scope of its practice rather than as a conscious movement. Developers such as Stuart Lipton and Godfrey Bradman, at King's Cross for example, are attempting the Community Architecture approach; Bradman is also behind an ambitious self-build housing programme, designed to put home ownership within reach of even the lowest paid or unemployed. Community architects are seeking links with other individuals and groups – outside their profession – who in some way represent New Age thinking and practice: the Greens, Friends of the Earth and other environmental pressure groups; those involved in preventive medicine and health care; and other like-minded souls in the other environmental professions. As projects become more numerous, so also they are getting bigger – often dealing with whole neighbourhoods or parts of cities rather than one-off buildings and designed within a framework of social and economic as well as physical regeneration.

Whole estates of local authority housing are now receiving the treatment. Identifiable areas such as Finsbury Park and Bishops Gate, the Vauxhall area of Liverpool and Derry within the city walls are benefitting from the Community Architecture approach, while more and more ambitious multi-professional teams are brainstorming at planning weekends, or 'charettes', to determine the future places such as Newcastle upon Tyne, Pittsburgh and Poundbury, with community involvement. As projects come on-stream, more research is being undertaken to assess users' needs and aspirations in advance of the first brick being laid; and then on completed schemes to establish whether these have been fulfilled. Empirical research is the order of the day and one of the leading practices, Hunt Thompson Associates, has set up its own subsidiary to carry out these tasks.

As proof emerges of the costliness of past architectural errors, and the cost-effectiveness of the Community Architecture approach – for example, up to five times as cost-effective in the provision of housing for the urban poor of the Third World – then yet more projects will be commissioned, and the research loop will be completed by feeding this information back into the schemes that follow. The growth of the Community Projects Fund, operated by the Community Architecture Group of the RIBA, to more than £70,000 a year, is proving to be a significant boost to getting new projects started, and many of the early beneficiaries have gone on to receive awards in *The Times*/RIBA Community Enterprise Scheme. And, as one community architect remarked recently, the movement is probably responsible for the best public relations the Institute has received in the last decade. As Community Architecture is not a style, however, is it architecture at all? Because the most publicised projects are basically refurbishments of existing buildings – Black Road phase one, Macclesfield, by Rod Hackney; and Lea View, Hackney, by Hunt Thompson – many believe that it is probably not. But that is a fallacy just as much as the notion that it is only concerned with housing, or with refurbishment. Many architects are community architects – occasionally – and examples of Community Architecture now include the award-winning rebuilding of a church and new health centre (Barnes Church and Lambeth Community Care Centre, by Edward Cullinan Architects), new community centres (Curry Mallet, by Joe Poynton of Poynton Bradbury Associates; and in Hackney, by Hunt Thompson) and scores of co-operative, housing association and self-build homes throughout the country, by a variety of practices.

The Community Architecture projects of two recent recipients of the Royal Gold Medal – Ralph Erskine, in 1987, and Renzo Piano, in 1989 – played a significant part in their nominations; while others, such as Giancarlo de Carlo, Lucien Kroll and the late Walter Segal have all achieved recognition for their work in this field. Community and Architecture are by no means mutually exclusive – in fact that would be a denigration of the role of the architect in the community. What community architects want is for users to be allowed to participate in the process by which architecture comes about. Those who have tried it, like Ted Cullinan at Barnes and Lambeth Community Care Centre, swear by it – saying that better architecture is the net result. The evidence exists for those who want to see it – so much for critic Martin Pawley's swipe, that it is no more than the 'evangelical wing of the home improvement market'! John Thompson's definition is that it is 'the architecture of reciprocal rapport'. Whether the product is tagged Hi-Tech, Post-Modern, Classical Revival, or any of the other derivatives beloved of critics is less important than whether it is 'firm, commodious and delightful' to those who use it.

While community architects struggle for recognition with their own professional peers, others have been quick to recognise the significance of the approach, irrespective of its stylistic trappings. Paul Ekins, an economist and leading member of the Green Party, called it the 'Greening of architecture', when he spoke at the Building Communities Conference three years ago. Many of us rather like that. While all around us seem to be pre-occupied with the stylistic expression of raw square footage, it does at least suggest that social idealism in architecture is not yet dead. But while Corb, Mies and Gropius had an unerring belief that technology (the machine) would provide most of the answers, including the creation of a more equitable society, we have the benefit of hindsight to tell us that is not so. Technology, though a useful means to an end, is a false god.

The fact remains that while architecture cannot shape the society we think we want, as the determinists would have it, the process by which it comes about leading to a better end product can indeed have a dramatic impact on those who have been involved and have to live with the result. Many people, the Prince of Wales included, know this almost intuitively. By creating a more responsive process, a more responsive product will emerge. Community Architecture might even be leading the way to a new consensus about what is good and what is bad architecture – in the eyes of both the profession and its public. In an age of pluralism, any style may flourish – but when has architecture ever been solely a matter of taste?

Notes

1 Charles Knevitt, *Community Enterprise*, *The Times* and Calouste Gulbenkian Foundation, 1986.
2 Bertha Turner, ed, *Building Community: A Third World Casebook*, Building Communities Bookshop By Mail, 1987; Richard Hatch, *The Scope of Social Architecture*, Van Nostrand Reinhold, 1984.
3 Nick Waites & Charles Knevitt,*Community Architecture: How People are Creating Their Own Environment*, Penguin, 1987.
4 Charles Knevitt, *Community Architect Mark I*, *Building Design*, July 11, 1975.
5 Jim Sneddon and Carloine Theobald, eds, *Building Communities: Proceedings of the First International Conference on Community Architecture, Planning and Design*, CAIS Ltd, distributed by RIBA Publications, 1987.
6 Charles Jencks, *Modern Movements in Architecture*, Penguin, 1973.

EDWARD CULLINAN, THE PARISH CHURCH OF ST MARY, BARNES, LONDON

HUNT THOMPSON ASSOCIATES
Bishops Gate

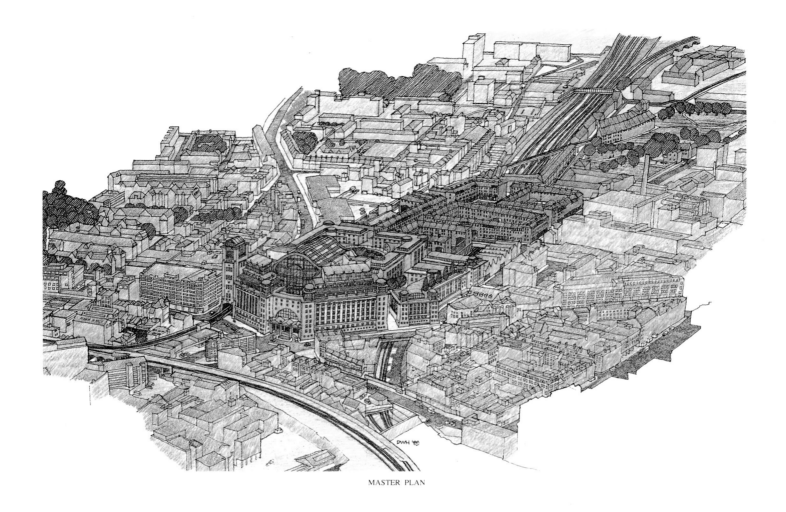

MASTER PLAN

Building upon our strong links with this part of London through our involvement in the Spitalfields Market Development, we have consulted the community in the preparation of our master plan. A Community Planning Weekend took place in January, extending the 'Planning for Real' exercise, an interactive process allowing communities to contribute to the planning of their environment. We believe that an understanding of the needs and aspirations of the community has been obtained. In order to forge a partnership between commercial and community needs, we propose that a Community Development Trust be formed, bringing together public, private and voluntary sectors in partnership, to carry out appropriate parts of the development.

We have sought to create an integrated development of office and business space, retail and leisure, workshop and studios, residential and community facilities, contained within a culturally and economically supportive community. Street life will be promoted with market areas and spaces for both formal and informal meeting, establishing appopriate senses of place. The architecture and uses of the scheme will create a background conducive to a spirit of physical and social well-being that has so often been found lacking in previous attempts to regenerate Inner Cities.

Analysis of the planning briefs provided by the community, the client, the owner and the local authorities has led us conclude that the site divides into three areas: West, fronting onto Shoreditch High Street; Central, between Wheler Street and Brick Lane; and East, between Brick Lane and Vallance Road. We believe that there should be a progression through these areas of decreasing density and scales of transition from commercial to community use and that all three should be actively linked and mutually supportive.

The West, anchored on the possible new three-way rail interchange, is the focus of a new office centre on the edge of the City. Strong links will be created with Broadgate and Spitalfields as well as the established business areas of the City. An important element of the process was the acceptance by the local community of the appropriateness of this area for commercial development.

The Central area will form a link between the commercial sections and the community-based uses. Provision will be made for new businesses, housing etc, contained within a traditional cityscape of streets and squares.

The East has been the subject of a separate study by McCormac Jamieson and Pritchard whose proposals, including the provision of new housing and community buildings, are in accordance with the Community Brief.

Planners: Hunt Thompson Associates;
Executive Architects: Covell Matthews Wheatley.

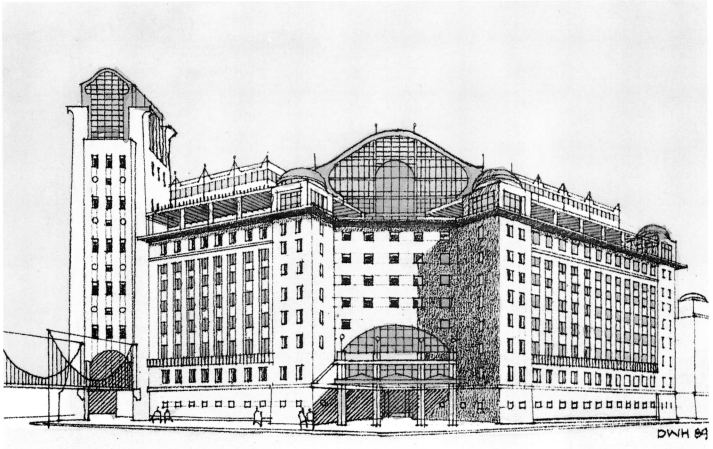

MASTER PLAN – WEST, *ABOVE*: NORTON FOLGATE; *BELOW*: SHOREDITCH HIGH STREET

41

Surrounding streets frame views – office mass never seen in its entirety. An appropriate incident for each view.
Drama of railway passing along and through new buildings, seen from Bethnal Green Road.

Campanile and bridge attract attention in maelstrom of traffic, southbound on Shoreditch High Street.

Wheler Circus ringed with restaurants, shops and cast iron columns from the Great Eastern Street viaduct.
Galleria and Atria provide natural light to deep-plan buildings.
Atria can be infilled for flexibility.
Variety of office floor plates.
Office buildings can be linked for flexible lettings.
Blocks to the south blend with smaller scale streets.

L to R: View along 18th-century Elder Street closed with buildings in traditional Spitalfields manner; Mounting scale from east to west, culminating in a Winter Garden poised astride the flagship building of commerce.

Streets and squares terminate in closed views.

Mothers' Hospital Project, Hackney

AERIAL VIEW

This is a large community project on the site of the Mothers' Hospital in Hackney. When the unit was transferred to new accommodation in 1986, City and Hackney Health Authority initiated plans for a new community mental health service, to be funded by proceeds from the sale of the site. The authority hoped to achieve this, not by moving into the established community, but by bringing the community into the hospital site. This has been achieved through partnership with community organisations and commitment by those involved to integrate mental healthcare with a variety of ordinary and special needs housing, in a traditional street setting. Hunt Thompson Associates have worked in conjunction with both the Health Authority and the purchasers, Newlon Housing Trust, to produce a combination of community housing and health care facilities, including shared-ownership flats for first-time buyers, rented and sheltered accomodation.

The project consists primarily of a three-storey terrace around a formal square. The architects have adapted a Classical style to create something surprisingly new; as Ian Chown of Hunt Thompson has said: 'We haven't attempted to make it a replica Georgian building. It's a 1980s building. We've avoided stucco because it isn't practical for our climate. We've gone back to Palladio's original principles.' The front elevation of the terrace is in keeping with the London idiom of brickwork, showing a gradation of colour from brown with a red stripe at ground level through London yellow, Kentish brown-yellow, and finally cream buff. The Doric and Ionic orders, symmetry, rustication and top-storey round-arched windows unite a varied community, creating a Classical scheme.

The 21 houses forming the terraces at the sides of the court are available for rent (though legislative changes have meant a substantial rise in prices, beyond the minimum 'fair rent').

The third and fourth phases of the project consist of sheltered housing for Newlon and a psycho-geriatric hospital for the Health Authority. Finally there will be the restoration and conversion of six Georgian listed houses in Maitland Place – the original frontage to the Mothers' Hospital – into 18 flats for rent.

Finsbury Park Project

This £30m scheme is designed for 10 acres of derelict railway sidings in Finsbury Park owned by British Rail and Islington Council. The idea for the project, to be realised by a Community Development Trust, was initiated at a public meeting in December 1987 to lodge overwhelming opposition to proposals made by CIL (City Industrial Ltd), the developers responsible for converting Islington's Royal Agricultural Hall into the Business Design Centre. The proposals of Sam Morris, head of CIL, had included road widening, a DIY warehouse and a shopping centre, as well as housing. This was not felt to be in keeping with the needs of the community. The Finsbury Park Community Forum was formed to work up counter proposals, bringing in the help of Hunt Thompson Associates, together with private sector (Unity Trust Bank) and Housing Corporation funding.

The planning brief which Hunt Thompson

AERIAL VIEW OF MODEL

had to work with, developed by the Community Forum, was to maximise the amount of rented housing, and to provide some housing to be sold on the open market. The detailed plan provides for over 200 homes, over a third of which will be for sale, with the rest a mixture of Housing Association, shared ownership and self-build; together with workspace and a garden centre running training courses for 25 unemployed young people. It is estimated to provide around 500 jobs in new workshops, and encourage new businesses.

The Prince of Wales has been a keen supporter of the project. In his capacity as president of Business in the Community, the Prince has said: 'It points to new and exciting ways in which the local community can become involved in developing its own environment . . . You are demonstrating the supreme importance of organisations working together to achieve success in the inner cities.'

COMMUNITY ARCHITECTURE
Compiled with the help of Maureen Read

LEA VIEW HOUSE, HACKNEY

Community enterprise, involving the active participation of community groups in controlling the development of their own environment and in determining the processes of planning and urban regeneration, has emerged as one of the most significant trends of the late 80s. As a movement encouraging the creative interaction between the community and the architect, Community Architecture has played a key role in the architectural debate, finding its most influential advocate in the Prince of Wales who has done much to establish its credibility within the architectural and critical professions. As Patron of The Times/Community Enterprise Scheme (now completing its fourth year), the Prince has been actively involved in promoting a variety of community projects ranging from self-build housing projects, to the repair and transformation of derelict and obsolete buildings to create community centres and workshops for new businesses, to the improvement of dilapidated housing estates, and the re-establishment of open spaces within the fabric of the urban environment. Below is a very small selection of recent projects solely to give an impression of what has been achieved.

ASHCOTT VILLAGE HALL, BRIDGWATER, SOMERSET
This project started as the result of a successful Village Jubilee weekend. With proceeds of £800 it was decided at an open meeting, that with the growing population of the village likely to exceed 1,000 people by the late 1980s a village hall would be a great asset.
The Old Church Rooms were purchased and a conscious decision made to retain the look of the Rooms by carefully blending old stone with the new reconstructed stone so as to tone in with the church and surrounding houses.
The most interesting feature of this small hall is a hydraulic stage, made by committee members to enable greater utilisation of the floor space. This hall, 65'x45' with a total cost of £110,000 has been a unique effort by a very small village to achieve their aims by working together.

LEA VIEW HOUSE, HACKNEY, LONDON E5
Lea View House, heralded as 'Heaven in Hackney' when it was opened in 1939, had, by the 1960s, become a run-down, hard-to-let sink estate hated by its tenants.
Out of sheer desperation, by the late 1970s, the tenants had forced their way onto the Council's priority list. Hunt Thompson Associates were appointed in Autumn 1980 with a brief to keep the tenants on the estate. They immediately set about establishing constructive relationships with the tenants, who both demanded and deserved genuine participa-

tion. A 6.5 million pound rolling programme, funded through Hackney Council has now reached near completion.

THE ELDONIAN NEIGHBOURHOOD REVITALISATION PROJECT
The Eldonian Community Association in Liverpool grew under a cloud of threat which hung over the community in terms of both employment and housing conditions. With the closure of the Tate and Lyle Sugar Refinery and the loss of many local jobs, came the added problem of how to resist Liverpool City Council's tenement clearance programme.
The Association secured two options for people wishing to remain in the community involving rehousing for people who wished to remain council tenants and new housing in the Portland Gardens Co-operative for others.
The co-operative produced a submission for the Tate and Lyle site ideas competition with co-operative housing and small industrial buildings for community business. The strength of the proposal persuaded the Government to grant £6.5 million to develop the site. The members of the co-op were able to determine the design of their homes through 'surgeries' with the project architects, Wilkinson Hindle Halsall Lloyd Partnership and visits to other estates. The Eldonian project won the top Times/RIBA Community Enterprise Award (1988) and the village was officially opened this year by HRH

Prince of Wales.

LIGHTMOOR NEW COMMUNITY PROJECT
Situated outside Telford in Shropshire, the Lightmoor project won the top Times/RIBA Community Enterprise Scheme Award in 1987.
 The concept was to create a mini- neighbourhood with its own work areas, housing and environmental management. Discussion workshops took place and a residents' group formed. Architecture students worked on designs for appropriate house styles. Conservation of the local countryside was an important consideration, along with the involvement of children in the design process of their own playground. The residents' group gradually developed into a formal community association. Funding was obtained to contribute towards the development of an educational resource service. Youth workshops have been established along with the 'Green Finger' Cultivation Project.

LEWISHAM SELF-BUILD HOUSING ASSOCIATION - PHASE II, WALTER'S WAY.
The architect Walter Segal pioneered the self-build housing method using timber frame construction. Experience has shown that D-I-Y skills can be easily mastered to build a house in this way from beginning to end.
The first scheme was granted permission in 1976, initiated by Segal and Lewisham council architect Brian Richardson. Members of the self-build group were previously on the council's waiting and transfer lists. No-one was prevented from joining because of low income, age or personal circumstances. Previous experience in building techniques was not a requirement.
Each family involved in the project was responsible for building their own house at their own pace, tailored to their own needs. The houses were built as 'council houses' with Lewisham paying for the materials. Once the work was completed each self-builder was sold a 99 year lease for half the value of the house. A council mortgage was then obtained with a reduction in repayment to compensate for labour and work imput. The remaining half share is owned by the council and the self-builders have the option to buy into the share in 10 per cent instalments.
The Walter's Way Project won a Times/RIBA Award in 1987.

ABOVE L TO R: ASHCOTT VILLAGE HALL, BRIDGWATER, SOMERSET; LEWISHAM SELF-BUILD HOUSING ASSOCIATION; *BELOW L TO R:* THE ELDONIAN NEIGHBOURHOOD REVITALISATION PROJECT, LIVERPOOL; LIGHTMOOR NEW COMMUNITY PROJECT, TELFORD

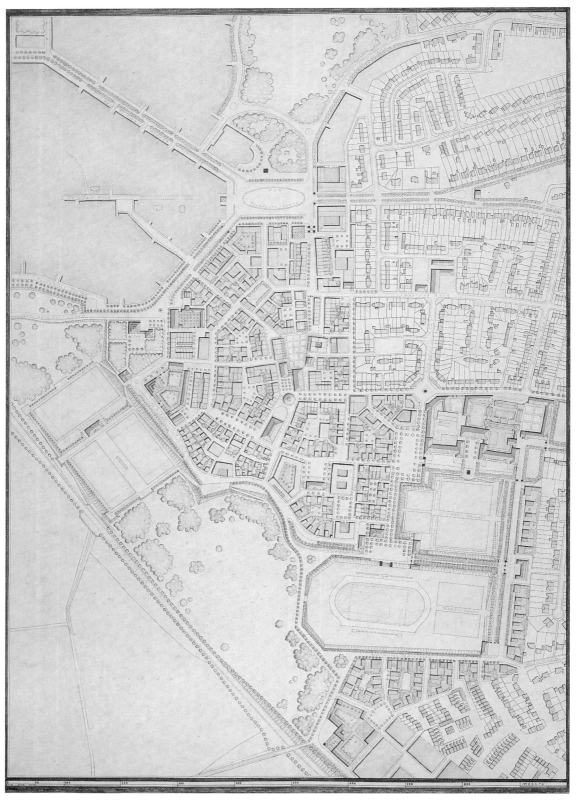

Plan of the first Middle Farm quarter. Above left: the new Poundbury quarters and Poundbury avenue leading towards the civic centre. Below right: the New West Dorset Leisure Centre forming large landscaped terraces between Middle Farm quarter and Castle Park. The extensions of Castlefield School and the leisure centre form a clear frontage to the streets, squares and sports fields. All car parking is along public avenues, squares and parades. The boundaries of the new quarter are formed by landscaped tree-lined promenades. The governors of Castlefield School have voted against a public square in front of their school and the residents of James Road have protested against a new row of houses fronting the leisure centre and their road being linked to these facilities. These objections to the plan have led to a major reappraisal of the siting and dimension of the first phase.

LEON KRIER
Master Plan for Poundbury Development in Dorchester

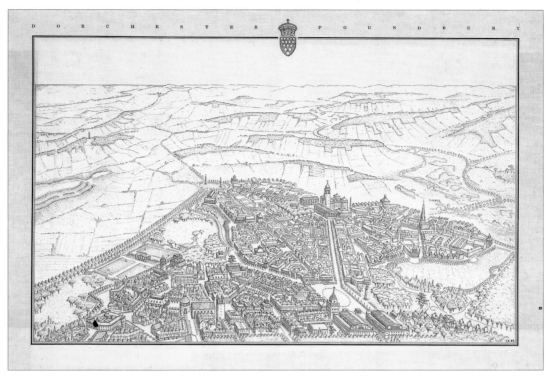

The Civic Centre and Watertower-Belvedere occupy the high ground around Poundbury Farm. In the foreground Middle Farm is separated from Poundbury by the relocated Bridport Parkway and a large common and cemetery on the right. The old Roman Bridport Road becomes the high street of one of the Poundbury quarters and the spectacular group of trees around Poundbury Farm will form a green in front of the Civic Centre.

Until 1800 the historic centre of Dorchester occupied an area of 100 acres and had 4,000 inhabitants working and living within its walls. Since then the Roman town has lost most of its residents and has instead been transformed into a shopping and administrative centre for a suburban population of 15,000 and for many villages beyond. This accounts for the profound changes of its historic building and social fabric, the transformation of fine houses, schools, workshops and churches into shops and offices, of its many gardens into car parks.

The urban area of Dorchester is over 750 acres and the Duchy of Cornwall's Poundbury development will allow the town to grow by 450 acres within the line of the new by-pass. To merely expand the suburban sprawl would overload the centre with more central functions and increase the problems of congestion, etc. In November 1988 the Duchy of Cornwall approached Leon Krier to elaborate in consultation with the local authorities and other concerned bodies a form of urban development which, rather than segregating urban uses as has been the trend for many decades, instead integrates all essential community needs and activities within several new urban districts, none of which exceed 100 acres.

Each of these districts is conceived of as a traditional Dorset town or village with a traditional street pattern and common, traditional building types and materials. Each section of development will be self-sufficient in education, employment, shopping, leisure. Those who seek employment will be able to find residential accommodation within five to ten minutes walking distance. Regular markets will be held within each district and most shopping needs satisfied without using the car.

Corresponding to the Dorchester District Council's wishes for the expansion of Dorchester to be phased over 10-15 years, the Duchy of Cornwall Poundbury development will, according to the master plan of Leon Krier, be articulated into four urban communities, of 500-800 households each, and none exceeding the 100 acres of the Roman town. It will take three to four years to complete one of these urban districts, corresponding to the desired growth of 200 households per year. While the first quarter, Middle Farm, will be an organic extension to the existing Cambridge Road suburb, three further urban districts will be built around Poundbury Farm; the groups of large trees acting as a central common. Bridport Road will be re-routed to form a tree-lined avenue, separating Middle Farm village from the Poundbury districts.

Architects and builders who have had a long experience in traditional design and construction will be selected to realise the actual buildings. And Andres Duany is drafting the urban building code which will ensure the faithful realisation of the master plan.

Masterplanner: Leon Krier
Assistant: Liam O'Connor

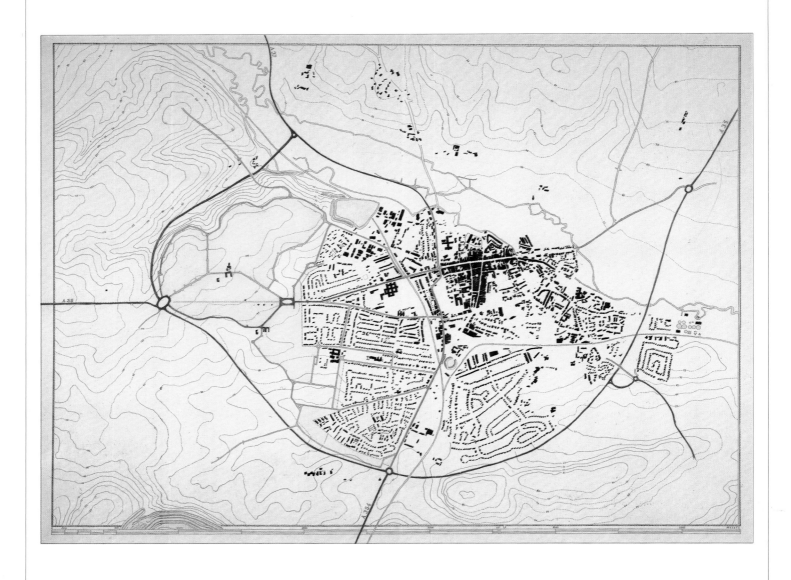

The existing urban fabric clearly shows the different natures of the historic town and the recent suburbs; without the historic centre the suburbs would collapse like a body severed from its head. They not only lack basic urban functions and work, but they are also very poorly connected to the Centre and even more poorly connected between themselves. Virtually 95 per cent of all the shopping facilities are concentrated within the Old Centre. Dispite the huge gaps between the main concentrations of buildings, the principal traffic routes disrupt the inner life of the central parishes of Dorchester and Fordington. In the new development, through traffic will be channelled between the new urban quarters.

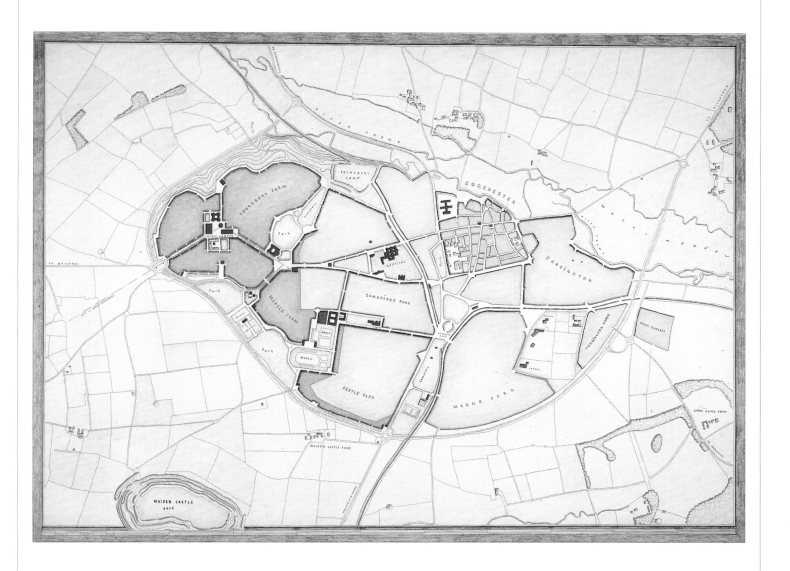

The location of the new urban quarters is defined by the topography of the site and by the shape of the existing suburbs. The first phase of development will be a rounding off of the existing Cambridge Road suburb, giving it a centre to relate to and clearly defined limits in the form of promenades and parades inspired by Dorchester's tree-lined south and west walks. The Castlefield School and the expanding West Dorset District Leisure Centre will effectively form a civic centre for the existing Castle Park, Victoria Park, Cambridge Road and the New Middle Farm quarters. Three new urban quarters will focus around the new Civic Centre, occupying the high ground on Poundbury Farm. Through traffic is channelled on the Boulevards dividing the new urban quarters. These form tree-lined avenues focusing on important natural features like Maiden Castle, existing monuments like Hardy's Monument, or on important institutional buildings to be located on the most prominent sites. Although the programme for such buildings is still not finalised, over the coming years the creation of these prominent sites will give to the town and County the opportunity to fulfil new needs. The county and district organisation, rather than adding onto existing buildings in the historic centre, will be able to expand into new buildings, enriching the life and fabric of the new quarters. An archives building, County court house, conference centre, hotel, church and further public functions will find appropriate locations here.

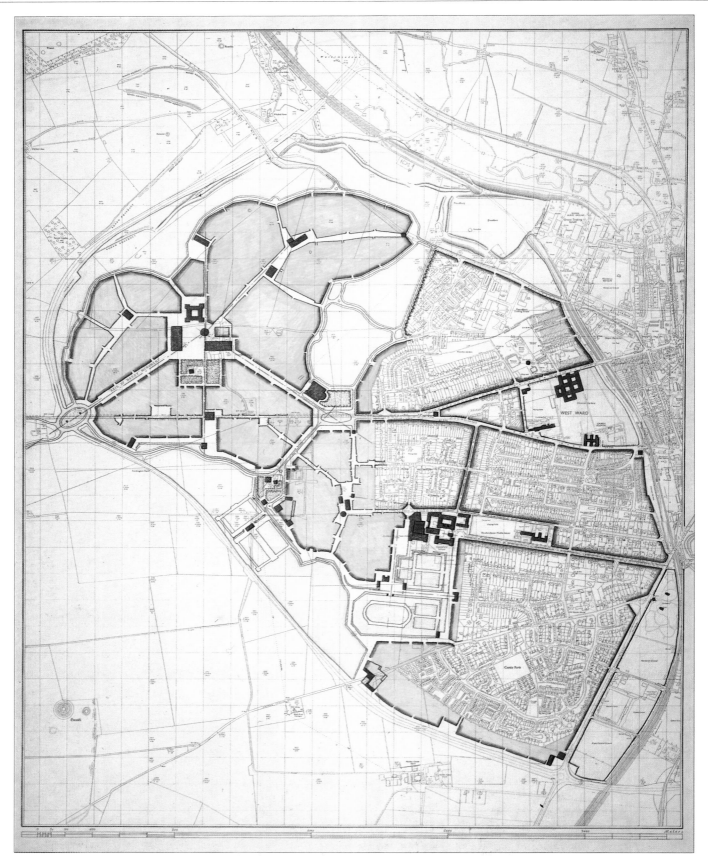

Plan showing boundaries of existing and new urban quarters; each quarter being a small town. Local functions are located on the central local squares, the high streets which connect them. and the civic centres around Castlefields School and Poundbury Farm. The latter will contain leisure, culture, education and administrative activities which are of interest and use to the entire city of Dorchester and to the Dorset County as a whole.

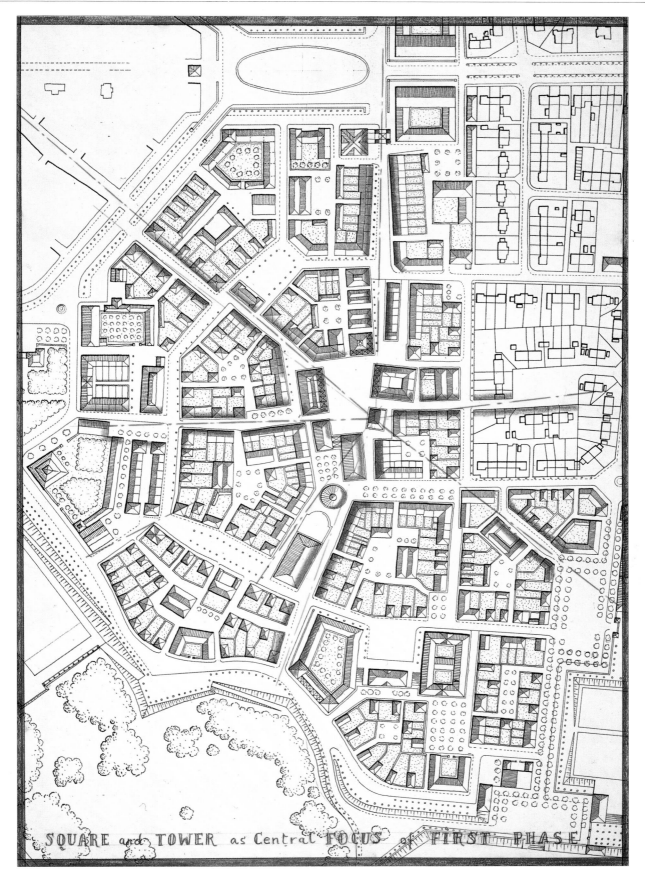

SQUARE and TOWER as Central FOCUS of FIRST PHASE

The Tower forms the focus of the Middle Farm quarter located on the central square. High streets radiate from this Civic Centre, reaching into the existing Victoria Park suburb, and leading to the public park or to the new Poundbury quarters, occupying the higher ground around Poundbury Farm.

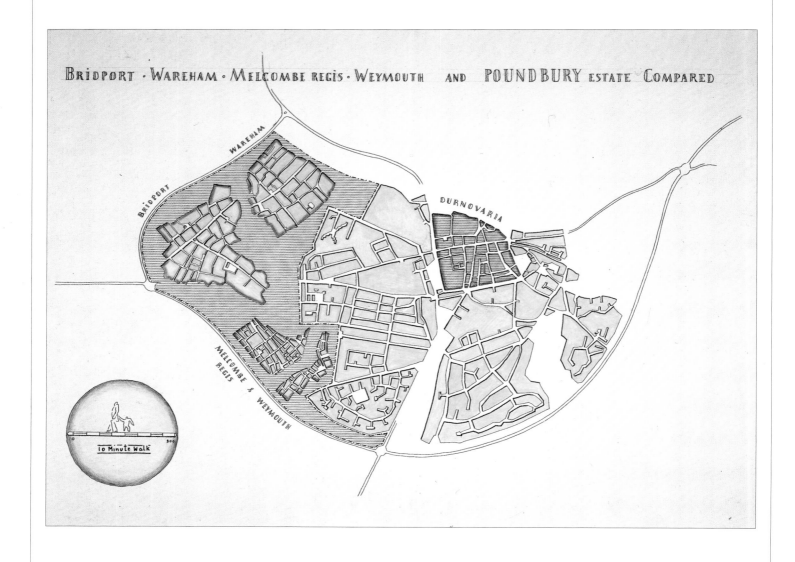

BRIDPORT · WAREHAM · MELCOMBE REGIS · WEYMOUTH   AND   POUNDBURY ESTATE COMPARED

10 Minute Walk

The Duchy of Cornwall estate (Poundbury and Middle Farm) within the New Dorchester by-pass occupies 450 acres of land. It is large enough to comfortably contain the historic centres of Wareham, Bridport, Wymouth and Melcomb-Regis. The entire historic centre of Siena, with all its gardens, olive groves, forts and 50,000 citizens, easily fits onto this site.

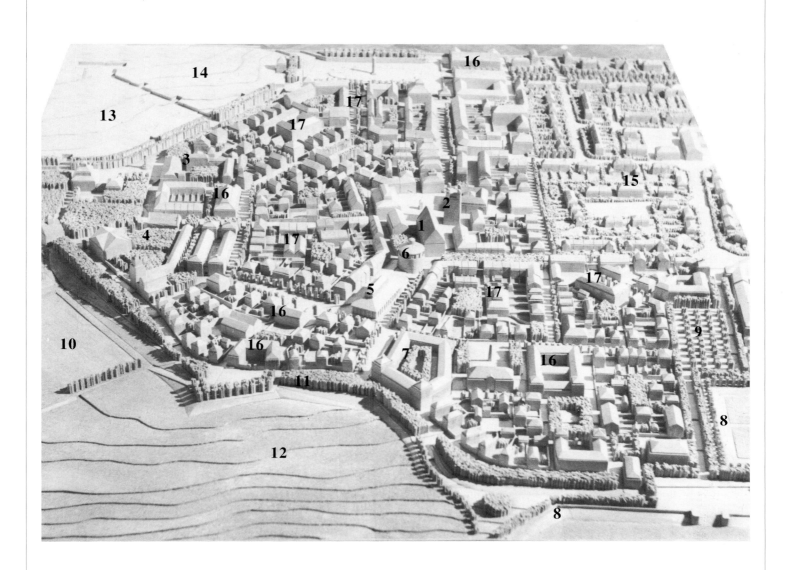

KEY

1 Civic Hall
2 Tower
3 Museum in existing Farm buildings
4 First School
5 Covered Market
6 Library

7 Hotel
8 Leisure Centre
9 Parking Squares and Avenues
10 Relocated Rugby Field
11 South Parade
12 Park

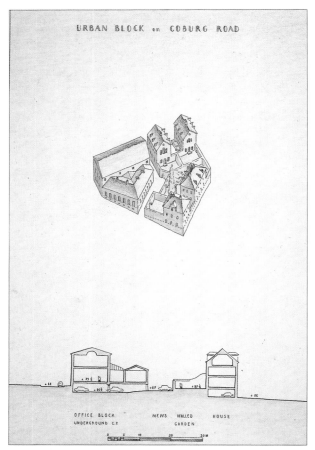

URBAN BLOCK on COBURG ROAD

OFFICE BLOCK   MEWS WALLED   HOUSE
UNDERGROUND C.P.   GARDEN

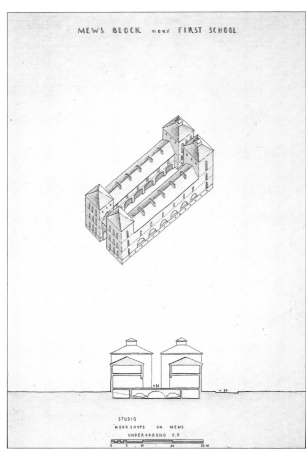

MEWS BLOCK near FIRST SCHOOL

STUDIO
WORKSHOPS ON MEWS
UNDERGROUND C.P.

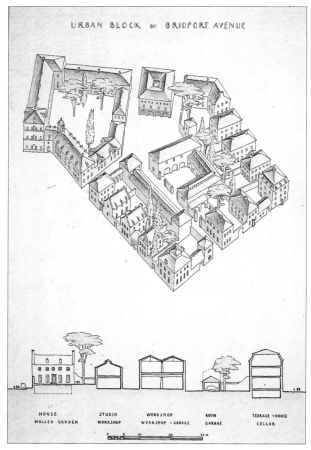

URBAN BLOCK on BRIDPORT AVENUE

HOUSE   STUDIO   WORKSHOP   ROOM   TERRACE-HOUSE
WALLED GARDEN   WORKSHOP   WORKSHOP-GARAGE   GARAGE   CELLAR

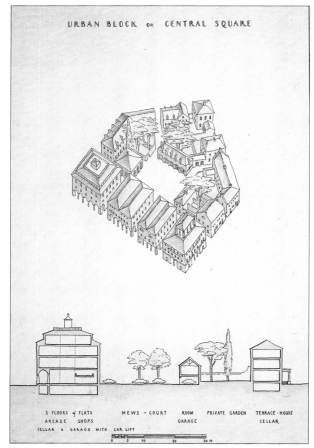

URBAN BLOCK on CENTRAL SQUARE

3 FLOORS of FLATS   MEWS-COURT   ROOM   PRIVATE GARDEN   TERRACE-HOUSE
ARCADE SHOPS   GARAGE   CELLAR
CELLAR & GARAGE WITH CAR LIFT

Urban Blocks

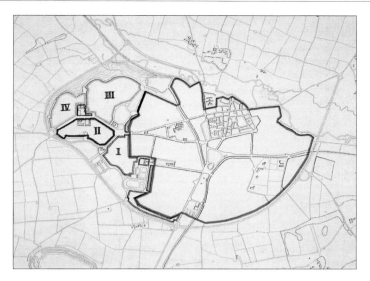

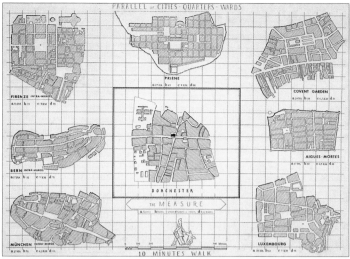

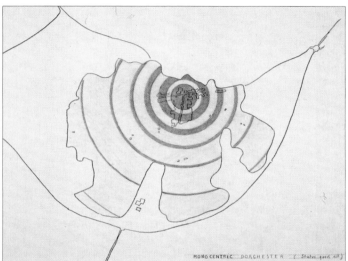

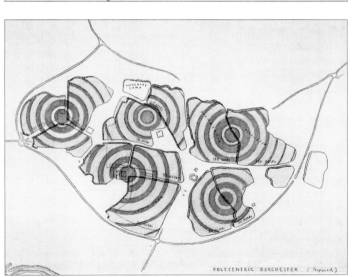

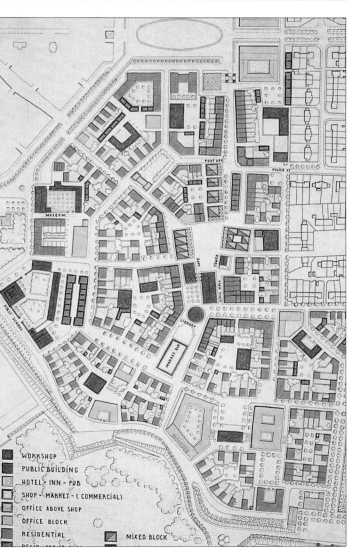

Above L to R: *Phasing of the Development; None of the 4 new urban quarters will exceed the 100 acres of historic Dorchester, here compared to important city foundations and urban quarters of the past;* Centre L: *Dorchester is now effectively a monocentric town based on the compulsive use of the private car;* Below L: *Dorchester as a polycentric town where most activities can be performed on foot;* Below R: *Mixture of uses within the Middle Farm quarter.*

LEON KRIER, BELVEDERE, SEASIDE, FLORIDA, 1988

CLASSICISM IN BRITISH ARCHITECTURE
Michael Collins

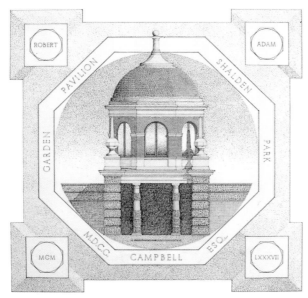

ROBERT ADAM, GARDEN PAVILION, SHALDEN PARK, 1987

In this brief survey of architects currently designing in the Classical idiom, Michael Collins discusses the pluralism of the 80s and the variety of ways in which individual architects are now interpreting the language and principles of Classicism, from the popular facadism of Quinlan Terry, through the conceptual urbanism of Leon Krier, to the community projects advocated by the Prince and the Post-Modern contextualism of Terry Farrell.

Classicism has more than once punched a hole into a preceding style, or itself been usurped by a counter-revolution. The Neo-Classicism of 1789 tore apart the soft frippery of the Rococo, with the latter's aristocratic associations. How many Classicisms and Neo-Classicisms are there? The architecture of Greece and Rome; the Renaissance; the Baroque; British Palladianism; the Neo-Classicism of the authoritarian left in France in 1789; the continuation of Classicism in the 19th century; its revival during the Edwardian free style; its submergence into the text of the great Germans and Austrians, such as Peter Behrens, Ludwig Mies van der Rohe, and Adolf Loos; its echoes in Le Corbusier; the totalitarian Classicism of Hitler and Stalin; the humanist tradition in the writing of Geoffrey Scott's *The Architecture of Humanism* (1914) and Rudolf Wittkower's *Architectural Principles in the Age of Humanism* (1949). The list goes on and on.

20th-century British Classicism has more than once taken an oppositional stance. Lutyens rebelled against the prevailing Arts and Crafts movement as early as 1894. He positively offended Dame Henrietta Barnett by producing neo-Georgian and neo-William and Mary houses for Hampstead Garden Suburb from 1908, going against her preference for Arts and Crafts architecture. A year later the architects Adshead and Ramsey began their progressive neo-Regency housing in Kennington for the Duchy of Cornwall; unveiled by the then Prince of Wales in 1914.

Classicism, and historicism in general, were sharply challenged by the International Modern of the 1920s. Some British architects, such as Sir Reginald Blomfield, retaliated by calling it 'modernismus'; he stated in 1935 that 'people will tire of what they cannot understand and artists will resume the standpoint that has guided art from time immemorial . . . one generation will see the end of this crazy movement'. He was, however railing against the intellectual tide, and failed to stop the erection of Connell, Ward and Lucas' brave white house of 1936 in his beloved Georgian and neo-Georgian Hampstead.

This 'Fog in Channel – Continent Isolated' viewpoint did survive, along with Classicism. The much praised country practice in Suffolk of Raymond Erith (1904-73) has been celebrated, not least because it fostered Quinlan Terry, who set up with Erith in 1962. Terry (born 1937) has been seen by some as a spearhead of fogey, new right Classicism, populist but painfully thin and even emasculated when compared with, say, Sir John Soane or Sir Edwin Lutyens. Terry's largest completed work is the Richmond Riverside development of 1988, a fashionable exercise in historically disjointed veneerism and facadism. The problem is that, in his new building for Downing College, Cambridge, of 1988, the Classicism is effete when tested against its juxtaposition with the earlier Classicism of William Wilkins for Downing of 1806.

The Thatcherite 1980s has spawned a Brideshead Revisited country house nostalgia boom, serviced by architects such as Roderick Gradidge, Julian Bicknell and Robert Adam. Gradidge (born 1929) has, for example, produced Classical restoration work in the context of Easton Neston. Julian Bicknell (born 1945) has, from 1984, produced an archaeologically correct Neo-Palladian villa, Henbury Rotunda, Cheshire, a new heritage house which replaces a destroyed one in an 18th-century land-

JEREMY DIXON, HOUSING AT COMPASS POINT, ISLE OF DOGS, 1985, RIVERSIDE VIEW, PAINTING BY CARL LAUBIN

scape park. Robert Adam (born 1945) is fascinated by Classical systems of proportion; his best building is Dogmersfield Park, Hampshire, of 1986, an expansive extension to a Georgian house. Dogmersfield sports the Tuscan order, but has windows without glazing bars, thus avoiding the troublesome but 'correct' sash window. Curiously, the Post-Modernist Robert Stern has criticised this gesture by stating that 'traditional windowpanes are scale-givers, which relate to the overall proportional system of a building, and to eliminate them is like replacing standard English brick with cinder blocks'. Other architects, such as London-based John Melvin, have produced urban houses based on Classicism. Melvin's houses at Brook Green are a case in point and he writes that 'it is from the ruins of a broken tradition that the retrievalists seek for their new forms and old truths'.

There is, however, a cutting edge to British Classicism. It is present in Community Architecture, Urbanism and Contextualism, and in the work of painfully few British Post-Modernists. Valuable too, is the polemical writing and work of non-indigenous architects such as Leon Krier and Demetri Porphyrios and the architectural fundamentalism of Islamic architects working here, such as El Wakil and Al-Bayati. It is also alive in the genius of Edward Jones, and the unclassifiable architecture of John Outram. The work of Abdel-Wahed El Wakil isn't Classical, but exemplifies another back-to-tradition stream. El Wakil was born in Cairo in 1943, and trained with Hassan Fathy in traditional Islamic architecture for five years; he has offices in Cairo, Boston and Ashford, in Kent. El Wakil quotes Fathy's statement that 'when the full power of human imagination is backed by the weight of a living tradition, the resulting work of art is much greater than any artist can achieve when he has no tradition in which to work or when he willfully abandons his tradition'. El Wakil's summer residence in Agamy, Egypt, of 1975 for Esmat Halawa, presses into service local materials such as sandstone

and marble, using alcoves, loggias, and domes to continue the Islamic tradition. A more pluralistic, less fundamentalist approach is taken by Basil Al-Bayati, who, though born in Baghdad in 1946, works from London. He is steeped in the history of Islamic architecture, and deeply inspired by Persian tomb-towers, Cairo Mosques, Moghul palaces etc. He is also, however, motivated by Western Classicism, in for example his project for Park Gate, London, drawn from the Classical ordering system of proportion, as well as the use of columns and mansard roofs.

Individual houses and buildings within the Classical and traditional system are one matter; more broad is the issue of the definition of Classicism, and its use within an urban context. According to Demetri Porphyrios 'Classicism is not a style'. Born in 1949 in Greece, he works in London, and has emerged as an academic Classicist, rigorous in his celebration of authentic true principles. He writes that 'architecture . . . is concerned with recurrent images that afford recognition of the world . . . the role of imitation and convention in architecture is to elicit that which is lasting and true for us from the transient'. Porphyrios' mastery of tradition is exhibited in his project for an extension to the Fitzwilliam Museum, Cambridge, of 1986, about which he has stated that 'the new extension to the Fitzwilliam Museum should be a testimony to the enduring values of the Founder's building'.

Perhaps the most brilliant polemicist within the Classical tradition is Leon Krier, born in 1946 in Luxembourg. He has been based in England, and worked with James Stirling from 1968 to 1970. More recently he has been involved with Classical reconstruction schemes for Washington D C and Berlin, almost echoing Loos' cry from the wilderness at the start of this century that 'at the beginning of the 19th century we departed from tradition . . . that is the point from which I want to continue'. His concerned writing on urban and social issues, his scheme for Spitalfields-Market redevelopment of 1987 and his plan for the

MISS WATT'S NEW CROQUET SHED, AYNHO

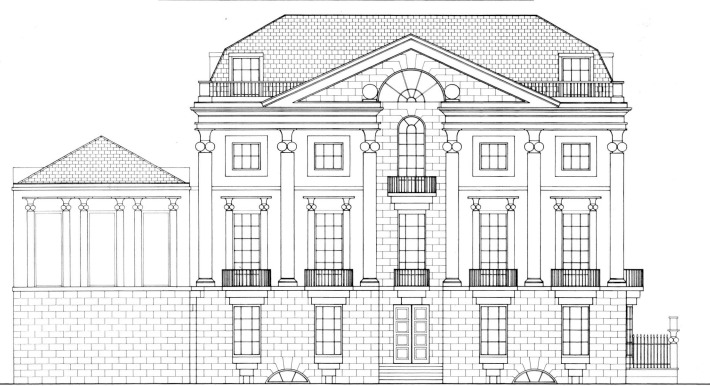

ABOVE: RAYMOND ERITH & QUINLAN TERRY, CROQUETTE SHED FOR MISS WATTS, 1987, DETAIL; *BELOW*: BASIL AL-BAYATI, PARK GATE RESIDENCE, 1989, FRONT ELEVATION

ED JONES, CITY HALL, MISSISSAUGA, 1986

new village near Dorchester for the Duchy of Cornwall have all brought him greater public attention in Britain, and the important ear of Prince Charles. His significance is still as a polemicist, and his only realisable project so far has been the Belvedere in Florida. Krier's visions are often given life in the splendid coloured drawings of Rita Wolff. Krier's lasting importance is in continuing the humanist tradition, in seeing the city in context as a sum of parts. Philip Johnson has assessed his contribution by suggesting that 'there are all kinds of architects, like Kiesler, like Ledoux, Krier, that become leaders without necessarily building. What Krier's done for drawing, for urban conceptualism . . . is enough for one man to create . . . his re-do of Washington: Boy! that is urban design . . . a man like Krier can vastly help form-making by focusing attention on the urban scene'.

Liam O'Connor (born 1961), who is currently working as assistant to Krier, having trained under the guidance of Demetri Porphyrios at the Polytechnic of Central London, is one of a group of younger architects drawn to the Classical idiom. His measured drawings, in which the Orders, proportions, materials and rustication are finely delineated in pencil and watercolour, form part of his student work, and include the drawing of a lighthouse on the island of San Giorgio Maggiore in Venice, designed by the Neo-Classicist Guiseppi Mezzani, 1810-15.

Community Architecture, supported by Prince Charles, has also done much to repair and restore, sometimes in a fragmentary way, while the Prince has chivalrously lanced 'monstrous car-buncles' and stated in 1988 in Pittsburgh that 'the most essential feature of this whole debate is how to re-create communities. At the heart of the question lies the human individual and how his surroundings are designed and laid out can make a huge differ-ence to his state of mind and to his behaviour'. Community Architecture has begun to be realised in, for example, Hunt Thompson Associates' Hindle House Community Hall renova-tion in Hackney, London. The soft approach to urban renewal has been demonstrated in the projects of architects admired by Prince Charles, such as Jeremy Dixon and John Simpson; both have used the Classical paintings of Carl Laubin to demonstrate colourful visions of their proposals for Covent Garden and St Paul's. Jeremy Dixon (born 1939) produced the hybrid Classical and Modern set piece of St Mark's Road Housing (1975-80) which is partly mimetic of the return to urban housing typology. His best known scheme is for the Royal Opera House extension, from 1983, which projects a re-creation of Inigo Jones-based arcaded buildings, confidently restoring the Piazza, and knitting in well with the fabric of the area. John Simpson (born 1954) has planned a Classical Revival scheme for Paternoster Square, near St Paul's, which takes on board the proximity and presence of Wren's masterwork. Simpson has expressed the view that 'it is only natural that we should turn to our heritage and tradition and, by building upon that, express ourselves as a society in much the same way as our forefathers always did in the past'.

Lastly, is there such an animal as British Post-Modern Classi-cism? Post-Modernism is prevalent in the approach of Terry Farrell, occasional to the work of James Stirling or Edward Jones, and debatable in the buildings of John Outram. Outram was born in 1934, and is somewhat of a rogue architect, in the best Victorian sense. His Harp Heating Headquarters, Swanley, Kent of 1983-85 involved the cladding of a 1960s dumb-box factory with a Classical outer shell, turning the glass box into a temple-like structure. One has suspicions; taking the famous Pugin line, and misquoting it, the result is 'All Modern, Sir; Classic details on a Modern body'. More convincing is Outram's daring The New House, Wadhurst, Sussex; it is a startling exercise in Neo-Palladianism and polychromy, partly in steel and concrete. It is a Neo-Palladianism much less literal and fun-damentalist than that of Bicknell, but not ironic enough to be

ABOVE: DEMETRI PORPHYRIOS, FITZWILLIAM MUSEUM, 1986; *BELOW*: JOHN SIMPSON, PATERNOSTER SQUARE, 1988, PAINTING BY CARL LAUBIN

ABOVE L TO R: MELVIN, BROOK GREEN HOUSING, 1986; EL WAKIL, AL QIBLATAIN MOSQUE, 1987; *BELOW L TO R*: FARRELL, COMYN CHING, 1978-85; BICKNELL, HENBURY ROTUNDA, 1984

fully Post-Modern. Outram's work can't be classified that easily, an example of British rogue elephantism, or what Voysey more politely cited as 'individuality'. Edward Jones on the other hand exhibits a quite welcome un-British approach to Neo-Rationalism. Jones (born 1939) and J Michael Kirkland (born 1943) have built the outstanding large-scale City Hall, Mississauga, in the Toronto suburbs. Completed in 1986, it sets up a resonance with the visionary Neo-Classicism of Claude Nicolas Ledoux, the continuation of Scandinavian Classicism in the 1920s architecture of Gunnar Asplund, the work of Aldo Rossi, and the visions of Leon Krier. He has also been influential as a teacher, at the Royal College of Art, London, and University College, Dublin.

The flagship of British Classicism is James Stirling's Neue Staatsgalerie, Stuttgart, of 1977-84, famous enough to feature in a recent advertisement for a British car. In 1986, Charles Jencks praised this building for being 'the most "real" beauty of Post-Modern architecture to date', though Stirling wrote in 1981: 'I don't think that our work attempts to be Post-Modernist'. Indeed he calls some parts of his gallery, (which also makes Classical and International Modern references) 'High-Tech'.

Most convincing as Britain's true Post-Modern Classicist is Terry Farrell. He was born in 1938, and became well-known for his Art Deco revival TV-am studios of 1982, and the Doric

Classicism of his Clifton Nurseries, Covent Garden, of 1980. Most excellent is his Henley Regatta headquarters of 1983-85; the boathouse typology of the Victorian era transmogrified into an almost American Post-Modern temple structure. He has evolved from these set-pieces to plan rich buildings in context, such as those for Comyn Ching, Monmouth Street, Seven Dials in London. As chairman of the Urban Design Group he has become absorbed with larger schemes such as the Hammersmith site for London Transport. He has in a practical way donned the mantle of urban renewal by producing excellent contextual projects for London. As a client of Farrell's said, he is the man 'who makes silk purses from sows ears', while he himself admits that his recent schemes 'respond to the more cautious taste of the banking/city world, as well as to their denser urban locations'.

In conclusion there are many types of Classicism. 1980s pluralism has encouraged traditionalism, fundamentalism, facadism, veneerism, toytown and doll's house Classicism, archaeological, pedantic and *rappel à l'ordre* Classicism, Community Architecture, urbanism and contextualism and ironic Post-Modern Classicism, to name but a few. If there is some jostling for position, perhaps more architects would do well to remember the old motto of all past Princes of Wales, *Ich Dien* (I serve). Architects can serve, without being servile.

LIAM O'CONNOR
Lighthouse in Venice, Measured Drawing

ELEVATION OF LIGHTHOUSE FROM THE SAGRATO

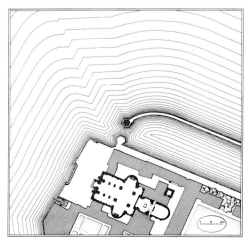

The Island of S. Giorgio Maggiore, with its Benedictine Monastery and church by Palladio, was made a Free Port in 1810. During the five years Giuseppe Mezzani built the harbour with its lighthouses at either end. Mezzani was a pupil of Giannantonio Selva and probably worked on his neo-classical Fenice Theatre in Venice (1790-92).

The lighthouses are situated like gateways to the harbour and complete the architectural composition of the Island buildings. The design owes much to the work of Michele Sammichele (1484-1559) - the Venetian Hawksmoor - whose fort at Sant'Andrea in Venice contains most of the compositional elements used by Mezzani, including horizontal bands of rusticated Istrian stone and keystoned window openings juxtaposed with rusticated arches. Each lighthouse is crowned with a chaste Greek - Doric monopteros

LOCATION PLAN, ISLAND OF S. GIORGIO MAGGIORE, VENICE

MAX HUTCHINSON
Inaugural Address to the RIBA

MAX HUTCHINSON, RIBA, JULY 1989

In this extract from his controversial speech as president of the RIBA, Max Hutchinson criticises the Prince's interventions. While acknowledging public resistance to change and the need for architects to recognise and respond to public opinion, he rejects the surface language and nostalgia of Post-Modernism and instead looks forward to the 21st century, advocating a reinterpretation of Modernist principles in the light of new technology.

There are many intermediate shades of opinion about current architecture and its future; but these are framed by two diametrically opposed views.

One school of thought is characterised by a kind of collective dread. Its manifesto says that the modern world is on a collision course, that the only principles worth aspiring to are those of the past; that the key to social stability is the reassurance of familiar forms and style. It is thus essentially backward-looking.

The other school of thought is characterised by hope. It says that the modern world is what we make it; that the principles of the Modern Movement (which sought to harness the power of technological impetus and innovation) have been obscured by paranoid introspection and the aesthetic pragmatism of the New Caroleans. This positive school of thought says that we must create a new age of discovery in which aspiration, instead of dragging us back, pulls us forward.

We were all born into the 20th century, a century which gave us, in its infancy, the theory of relativity, 12-tone music, Cubism, Ulysses, Marxism and the Bauhaus. We are now at the turn of the century and most people are still baffled by these ideas. The velocity of time itself has meant that we are constantly struggling to keep up with changes; struggling to understand a world evolving under our feet. The styles and techniques of Modernism may have been shunted off to some cultural siding, but the universal faith in the future which they engendered is still there, dormant, latent, waiting for a new impetus. The worst crime of Modernism was that of naivety. Modern architects were struggling to realise building forms beyond their time.

The intervention of the Prince of Wales has made honourable that which would have been considered cowardly half a century ago, namely the renunciation of the new in favour of the old. It underpins an image of the past with which the British are constantly caricaturing themselves. For now, as we enter the last decade of the 20th century, nostalgia is what it used to be. It is no longer enough that new urban developments respect the vestiges of 18th-century Britain; they must mimic them. It is no longer enough for social housing to be built in a form expressive of the materials used; it must be made to look like private housing, and why not, complete with clipped-on, jokey, quirky symbols of a Post-Modernism which has become both humourless and irrelevant, flaunting an imagination as desolate in execution as in purpose. Articulated by an heir apparent with the common touch and administered by a planning system which prefers formulae to ideas, popular taste demands reassurance, not challenge.

Richard Rogers is, for the Royalists, perhaps the most dangerous living architect. He is openly critical of the Prince's intervention. He is a brilliant architect. He is an outspoken champion of Modernism. And, most dangerous of all, he is popular. Ordinary people, to the great discomfort of some, like his work. Despite the campaign of vilification which has dogged Rogers throughout his career, whipped up by fogeyish architectural critics who pray for the first sign of rust on the silver, his architecture rallies popular support. His Lloyd's building is not only the most exciting new structure in London's urban landscape since the war; it also attracts up to 2,000 visitors a day. In five years it has become a national institution.

Despite what some of Prince Charles' supporters may claim, architects are not environmental pastry chefs. Our task is to create the spaces, both internal and external, which define our towns and cities. The misconception of architecture as 'appliqué' has been reinforced over the last few years by the nature of the debate. It has been all about the 'look' of much of our new development. In attacking the quality of new building, and especially new urban building, the Prince of Wales has attracted a large measure of support. But the criticisms of the anti-Modernists are based almost entirely on the appearance of our built environment, not on how it functions. The users of these buildings are simply not part of the equation. The argument, for many of the Prince's supporters, begins and ends with the contribution that an individual building – that is, the outside of it – makes to its surroundings. This is certainly a legitimate area of concern for both architects and the people they serve, for everyone is a consumer of buildings, whether they like it or not. Unlike music or painting, a film or a play, architecture is mandatory, public and unavoidable. For this reason alone, architecture must mind its manners. It must commend itself to the passers-by as well as serve its inhabitants.

The signal being given by reactionary forces in the architectural debate is that if things must change, they must at least not be seen to change. But a large Victorian building was not designed to accommodate modern requirements. When a new building is designed, it is created from the inside out; artistry, budget, consultation and function will determine the internal spaces, generate a plan, turn brief into form. A building of integrity expresses its character in its outward appearance. With contemporary, popular 'facadism', you are working in reverse; the datum is a two-dimensional external wall, often a piece of architectural jetsam rescued and re-used, quite brazenly, to barricade the past against an assault by the present.

Where no originals exist, it seems necessary to create them. Garden centres and DIY stores that look like the Crystal Palace are *de riqueur*. And when we are not replicating the originals, we are dressing up modern buildings with anachronistic bits and pieces from another century; a 19th-century arch is built into the wall of a reception area in the City of London; a Georgian crypt discovered during excavations is rescued and rebuilt, stone by stone, as a carpet-tiled marketing suite. We pin remnants of the past onto our urban fabric like antique brooches.

The *fin de siècle* we are heading towards has immeasurably more significance than most because it marks the threshold of a new millennium. Architecture, in common with all art forms, will discover a unity of purpose as we near the year 2000. The festivals of the past will pale beside the global celebration the new millennium will inevitably occasion. However, we simply cannot go to the Millennium Ball wearing the threadbare rags of Post-Modernism and Neo-Classicism. By the mid-1990s, a fresh architectural debate will be roaring over the kinds of built forms we want, both to take us into the 21st century and to leave behind as symbols marking the last decade of the second millennium.

The contemporary fashion for disguising the uncompromising forms of the Modern Movement can only partially succeed. Covering the South Bank with retail marzipan and icing cannot hide the original purity of inspiration. Modernist architects in this country over the last two decades have been not dead but simply dumb, circumspect. Post-Modernism, as its very name suggests, is an aberration, an absence of being. If rational and universal truths exist in architecture, we need to state them now.

Buildings of the early 21st century will demand to be more flexible and adaptable. So then, should we. If we are to be a Britain of vision we must agree to disagree about the past. We can love or hate Victorian Gothic or prefabricated 1960s high rise. The argument is historical. But we must achieve a consensus on the future.

One of the Prince's favourite examples of modern architecture – and one of mine – is Michael Hopkins' Stand at Lord's. It is simple, elegant and thrilling. The stretched-roof structure shows great skill and imagination in its design and is a testament to the freshness that technological ideas have beyond their time; for Buckminster Fuller and Frei Otto were pioneering stretched-roof systems 30 years ago.

We must not repeat the mistake of imagining that there can be a revolution overnight in the way that people regard new technology and new materials. There is a natural resistance to change in Britain which must be acknowledged. The modulation of built forms from the familiar and vernacular of the second millennium, into the new and contemporary third millennium must be taken at a pace which does not leave people gasping for breath. The Neo-Modernist revolution must be Fabian in character. And the change must also be part of an international movement which looks up from the national huddles of vernacular styles to a new colloquialism; the world colloquialism of a satellite age.

Thankfully, the task now is not to build on bomb sites and slum-clearance areas in the old sense. Rather we must repair or tear down the new slums and rebuild our cities, not in deference to history, but in anticipation of it. There is a growing feeling among young architects that our ideas have become static and outdated. They have no interest in the inherited guilt of the late Modernists. They want to build and to find forms that reflect a new reconciliation between art and science. A new interpretation of Modernist principles is needed, one which performs the role that architecture has always performed in bringing the benefits of an industrial revolution to the ordinary home.

Forget Post-Modernism. It was a welcome attempt to brighten up a Britain on the dole; a Britain which was taking less and less interest in its appearance and needed to get smart. It was architecture for consumers. Now we need a new architecture; a new Modernism, a Neo-Modernism, for the new producers. There's nothing new under the sun; it has to be neo. But if the choice is to be between bowing and scraping our way backwards with a Neo-Classicism which ignores new technology, or rediscovering economies of scale with new materials and new techniques aimed at sheltering everybody, I say let the cause be Neo-Modernism.

. . . We all have to live and work in the buildings that architects design, and under the laws that politicians frame. I firmly believe in the creative, competitive tensions that force both professions to respect the values of the society in which they live. Leadership, yes, but by consent.

This is the language of evolution, not revolution . . . It is a prosaic language – a language of compromise and moderation. It recognises that people change slowly and it respects their natural conservatism. But it is not the language of yesteryear. It has nothing to do with clinging blindly to the past. The architect must persuade by example – by the evidence of his work. For change to gather pace the pacesetters will have to encourage further changes and the acceptance of it. Of course there is conflict, as one style gives way to another. This is how it should be . . .

Let us regain the pride in our buildings that our forbears enjoyed. Let us hope that history may judge them favourably and let people develop for them an affection and an admiration that lasts over time. Above all, let the partnership of patron and architect flourish. For it is from this fusion of talent, temperament and realism that great buildings spring. **from the accompanying speech by the Rt Hon Michael Heseltine MP**

RICHARD ROGERS
Pulling down the Prince

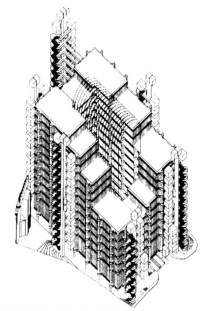

RICHARD ROGERS, AN EARLY VERSION OF THE LLOYD'S BUILDING

Richard Rogers is widely regarded by architects, critics and public alike as the most serious critic of the Prince's involvement in architecture. In his recent *Times* article, reproduced here, Rogers not only continues the debate, forcibly arguing for a new Modernism that responds to the realities of the urban environment, but goes beyond it to question the propriety of the Prince's interventions and his claims to represent unanimous public opinion.

In his sweeping criticism of Modernism, the Prince of Wales has failed to recognise that architecture mirrors society; its civility and its barbarism. Its buildings can be no greater than the sense of responsibility and patronage from which they originate. In blaming the architect and the architect alone for the ugliness of our built environment, the Prince exonerates the real culprits, thereby frustrating the very debate he wishes to encourage.

At the heart of the Prince's position is the claim that 'our age is the first to have seen fit to abandon the past'. This is, to say the least, an eccentric interpretation of the history of architecture, ignoring as it does the great turning points in the course of Western architecture, for example the eclipse of Gothic forms by the Renaissance.

Indeed, if there is any continuity at all in architectural history, it lies not in some illusory aesthetic, but in the fact that all departure from tradition has provoked ferocious controversy and opposition. When the first caveman left the shelter of his solid, waterproof, easily defensible cave for the light-weight, flexible, hi-tech hut (where one couldn't even draw on the walls) he was no doubt stoned for being a revolutionary with no feeling for social and visual tradition.

If the conservative principles favoured by the Prince of Wales and his followers had been applied throughout history, very little of our 'traditional' architectural heritage would ever have been built. Most of the great buildings in the Classical and Gothic traditions which the conservationists now value so highly were, in their own time, revolutionary. If the height of a new building had to conform to those around it, the great Gothic cathedrals

would never have seen the light of day. Likewise, the massive Italian stone *palazzi* of the 16th century, which today can seem the very exemplar of 'traditional architecture', dwarfed the one and two-storey wooden medieval buildings surrounding them.

When, three years ago, the Queen opened the new Lloyd's building, the Dean of St Paul's reminded me of the opposition that Wren had met with in the construction of St Paul's. Apparently he had to build a wall 18ft high around the site to prevent his critics from seeing and once more frustrating his plans. Several earlier designs had been blocked, including his 1673 design, of which the 'Great Model' can still be seen in the crypt of the cathedral. This is a magnificent project, and had it been built it would have been not only one of the greatest of all baroque masterpieces, but also one of the most technically advanced constructions of its time. Sadly, the design was too radical, the project was rejected, and in its place Wren designed the present less innovative cathedral.

If buildings like the great Gothic churches, the *palazzi* of Renaissance Italy or St Paul's seem to us to exist in a harmonious relation with their neighbours, it is not because they slavishly imitated them in size, style or material. Rather they embodied new building techniques and distinctive architectural forms quite unlike anything ever seen before. The contextual harmony that they seem to us to enjoy with their surroundings is the result of the juxtaposition of buildings of great quality, clearly and courageously relating across time.

I believe that the new movements in architecture that sprung up around the turn of this century represent an important turning point in the history of architecture comparable to that other great watershed, the development of the Classical forms of the Renaissance. Like the beautiful buildings by Brunelleschi or Wren, the designs of Sullivan, Le Corbusier and Mies van der Rohe offer a new aesthetic responsive to the scientific and ethical movement of the times.

Although you would not know it if you listened to the Prince of Wales, the Modern Movement, or at least a great part of it, represented a return to Classical principles. It emphasised the integrity of building materials, and it insisted, in contrast to the Victorian preoccupation with historical styles and with surfaces, that architecture was primarily concerned with the relation of three-dimensional form, with the play of light and shadow, of space and mass, rather than with ornament.

Together with these aesthetic principles went certain social commitments. The history of 'Modernism' had as its starting point the disastrous growth of the 19th-century city, and the spread of slum dwellings. Early efforts in modern design were marked by a concern to develop healthier, greener and more humanitarian environments; English garden cities and new towns reflect this reformist spirit. To the early Modernists architecture was not just another money-making business. They sought, in this architecture, to give expression to democratic ideals, to create new public forums and to contribute to freer and more egalitarian ways of living. Thus from its beginnings Modern architecture has been most interested in the design of houses and public institutions like schools and town halls and not, like its predecessors, in the construction of churches and palaces.

These Classical principles and progressive social commitments were given a revolutionary embodiment in the buildings of the early Modernists. For example, the discovery of relative space, manifest in the Cubist art, was given architectural expression in a greater abstraction of form; in particular, the newly evolved steel-frame structural system was used to free the walls of a building from load-bearing function, allowing greater freedom in plan and elevation. The possibility of high-density buildings, including the high-rise, was explored as a means of putting a halt to the spread of the suburb into the countryside and creating sunnier, more spacious homes, at a time when cholera was endemic in the cities and the brick back-to-back house was a symbol of deprivation, not rose-tinted nostalgia. And the democratic promise of mass production was celebrated by the employment of industrial components not only in factory buildings but in furniture sand houses.

Also like the architecture of the Renaissance, the buildings of the Modern Movement have proved to be not only visually and technically exciting, but capable of existing in a profound harmony with their man-made and natural environment. The Prince of Wales has argued that 'architectural adventurousness, producing non-traditional, exciting designs is certainly inappropriate in rural areas'. If applied to history this would, of course, have ruled out the work of Palladio or Vanbrugh. But even in the context of the Modern Movement, any one who has seen Frank Lloyd Wright's Fallingwater, Mies' Farnsworth House for Alvar Aalto's Villa Mairea, for instance, will know just how absurd it is to suggest that modern 'adventurous' architecture is incapable of harmonising with its natural setting.

The same is true in the case of the city; buildings like Mies' Seagram Building, Wright's Guggenheim Museum, and Roche and Dinkeloo's Ford Foundation, all in New York, prove that modern architecture can respond to an urban context in a manner that has never been surpassed. Fortunately, Britain is not without modern urban buildings that relate to their situation with a similar sensitivity; Sir Denys Lasdun's Royal College of Physicians, Alison and Peter Smithson's Economist Building in St James', YRM's own head-quarters in the City, and Darbon

and Dark's Limington Garden Housing Estate in Victoria, are some examples in London.

From its beginning, Modern architecture, like its Classical forerunners, has been concerned to incorporate new technology into its designs. Its best buildings have been infused with a spirit of innovation and discovery; they have celebrated the technology with which they are built. The excitement of a technologically adventurous architecture is evident in such modern masterpieces as Paxton's Crystal Palace, Frank Lloyd Wright's Johnson Wax Factory in Wisconsin or Norman Foster's Hongkong and Shanghai Bank.

Today we are living through a period of enormous scientific and technical advance; perhaps a second industrial revolution which offers architects an extraordinary opportunity to evolve new forms and materials. The computer, micro-chip, transputer, bio-technology and solid state chemistry could lead to an enhanced environment, including more rather than less individual control and fewer uniform spaces. The best buildings of the future, for example, will interact dynamically with the climate in order to better meet the user's needs. Closer to robots than to temples, these chameleon-like apparitions with their changing surfaces are forcing us again to rethink the art of architecture.

Architecture will not gain by clamping onto these technologically sophisticated constructions, a collage of disposable symbols like decomposed Classical columns, pediments and cornices, or flimsy Gothic turrets and Egyptian palm trees. Yet this Disneyland approach is what the Prince of Wales and his followers would seem to favour.

The rigid Classicism espoused by some revivalist architects and favoured by the Prince is particularly inappropriate for modern buildings. Classicism is based on the Vitruvian principle that architecture is about creating a building of 'rational' proportions every bit of which has its fixed size and shape so that nothing can be added or taken away without destroying the harmony of the whole. Thus the Classical style is quite unable to accommodate any alteration in the building's form. But the use and form of modern buildings change dramatically over short periods of time. A set of offices today might become an art gallery tomorrow; a perfume factory may switch to making electronics. And quite apart from the fact that buildings must be able to expand and contract, and change their function, a third of a typical modern office is occupied with technology which will need to be replaced long before the building itself needs to be demolished. All this makes flexibility an essential feature of effective modern design, and renders the Classical style quite impractical.

In contrast to the Prince of Wales' historicist architects, who are besotted with a past that never existed, I believe in the rich potential of modern industrial society and my own architecture has sought to respond to the needs of modern institutions by employing the most up-to-date scientific developments and exploiting the visual excitements that is inherent in them. My firm's design represents a search for an aesthetic which recognises that in a technological society change is the only constant; an aesthetic which allows some part of a building to be added or altered without destroying the harmony of the whole composition. The Lloyd's building illustrates our approach; it is intended to create a balance between permanence and change; its flexible elements – lifts, internal walls, air-conditioning and so forth – permit improvisation within a determinate whole.

Despite its achievement in the past decade, and its future potential, Modern architecture has been exposed to a barrage of criticism. It is paradoxical, to say the least, that at a time when the public has expressed a dramatically heightened interest in Modern art, and the value of paintings by the Modern masters has been exploded, the comparable movements in architecture should come under such sustained attack. Is it coherent to extol the Cubism of Picasso and Braque, while castigating its architectural counterpart in the architecture of Corbusier? Many of the critics of Modern architecture now seem to advocate the view that whereas art should be innovative and demanding, supplying new insights into our predicament, architecture should make us feel comfortable with ourselves and the nation we belong to.

The critics of contemporary architecture actually form a very diverse crowd, but while finding little else to agree on amongst themselves they are united on one point: they all claim to speak for the man in the street. It has now become an axiom, unquestioned by either its detractors or its defenders, that Modernism is loathed by the public.

My experience arising from the work of my architectural practice has been very different. More than five times as many people enter the Pompidou Centre every month as had originally been predicted: 70 million visitors in ten years, more than the combined total of visitors to the Eiffel Tower and the Louvre.

The National Gallery competition in 1982 drew immense public interest and our project, though uncompromisingly modern, gained the highest number of public votes, both for and against! Just as many people go to see the interior of Lloyd's (up to 2,000 per day), as visit many of our national museums. What then of the public's antipathy towards Modern architecture?

This unfounded view that all modern architecture is unpopular is, of course, closely associated with the Prince of Wales. The Prince's contribution to the architectural debate and his intervention in a number of important competitions and public inquiries has been given extensive and often enthusiastic media coverage, but what has been the impact of his involvement?

The Prince's apologists argue that his opinions reflect those of his subjects – the silent majorities – and that his interventions, despite appearances, are thoroughly democratic. Certainly the process by which planning decisions are made is of a forbidding, Byzantine complexity and probably needs reforming. Nevertheless, this slow, expensive, often obscure, haggling between different interests groups – commercial and environmental, national and local – is a rough, if flawed, approximation of democracy. Most of the participants of this process and the decisions they reach are ultimately accountable to one electorate or another; the Prince answers to no one.

The Prince is an advocate of community architecture and he claims that he wished to see greater openness about the way planning decisions are made; but his own conduct contradicts the public stand. He has, for example, proved rather shy of public debate. On several occasions critics and architects have accepted invitations to participate in a public discussion with him; unfortunately he has always declined to attend. Despite his well-publicised outbursts and his recent television programme, the Prince prefers to exercise his new-found prerogative as the nation's supreme aesthetic arbiter more surreptitiously, by paying secret visits to developers of important architectural projects or talking privately with the juries of major competitions.

In a similar manner we are assured that the Prince's judgements are not amateur or uninformed because he has gathered around himself a royal council of architectural 'advisers'; however, he will not publicly disclose the identity of these secret courtiers. Perhaps these inconsistencies point to a deeper contradiction in the Prince's stand. The claim to be defending a democratic approach to architecture does not sit easily with his own inherited authority. The Prince might consider whether the charges of paternalism and unaccountability, with which he criticises architects, might not more aptly be directed towards his own way of doing things.

Lest it be argued that the Prince's interventions are never decisive and therefore not undemocratic, I can cite the important competition for Paternoster Square in the neighbourhood of St Paul's Cathedral. This was probably the first international competition set up by a developer to judge a commercial development in London. The jury – including some distinguished architects and critics – selected two winners: Arup Associates and my own firm. The effect of the Prince's (secret) intervention was that we were asked to resign.

The Prince's intervention was even more dramatic on two earlier occasions: Mies van der Rohe's designs for Mansion House and Ahrends Burton and Koralek's extension for the National Gallery. In both of these cases there is little doubt that the Prince's public outbursts determined the outcome of the relevant planning inquiries. Neither does the prince show any sign of curbing his undemocratic intervention in the system of public inquiries he professes to admire. In his birthday television programme last year, the Prince criticised James Stirling's design for the Mansion House site with the barb that it looked like a 1930s radio; the Prince knew that the planning inquiry concerning this scheme was at a crucial moment in its deliberations and must have intended to effect its outcome.

No doubt the Prince's influence is usually less direct than it has been on these occasions; however, this only renders it more invidious. Rather than risk incurring the disapproval of the heir apparent, architects and their clients now try and guess the Prince's preference, submitting self-censored designs that they hope will meet with his approval.

For example, the Prince's 'carbuncle' outburst and his preference for Classical Revival architecture signalled to the organisers and competitors of the second National Gallery competition that Modern architecture should be excluded from the short list and so pastiche ruled the day. The office of I M Pei, well known for its Modernist designs, entered artfully rendered drawings of a Neo-Classical mausoleum. This contrasted with its design for the entrance to the Louvre a couple of years later, for President Mitterrand: a simple abstract pyramid using the most refined form of glass and steel technology available to create a sophisticated, contemporary building. We must assume the differences between the two buildings reflect the foreigner's view of the respective tastes of England and France.

While claiming to advocate a democratic architecture, the Prince's outbursts have generated a spate of mock-imperial palaces. One needs only to look at the ambassador's residence in Moscow, of all places. There the jury has made Britain a laughing stock by choosing a 'a show piece for Britain', a Classical pastiche. Britain's contribution to a new epoch in East-West relations looks like a stage set for *The Three Musketeers.*

Time and again the Prince has singled out individual architects for criticism; in doing so he is violating the principles of a constitutional monarchy. The Prince should keep his views at a general rather than personal level. Criticising individual architects, after all, is not any different from criticising individual doctors, lawyers, teachers or even politicians. It is particularly regrettable, however, that those whom he singles out – Professor Colin St John Wilson, Sir Denys Lasdun and James Stirling – are internationally acknowledged to be amongst our very best architects. They are also some of the few British architects who have avoided the large commercial schemes which have been the ruin of so much of our environment. In fact Wilson, Lasdun and Stirling have been amongst the most vocal critics of the quality of British architecture long before the media jumped on this issue. By singling out these influential architects, the Prince has wasted the opportunity to involve them in a constructive and non-partisan campaign to improve architectural standards.

Jettisoning the idea that the Prince's intervention in architecture is somehow democratic, his supporters sometimes argue that he has outstanding personal qualities which especially qualify him for involvement in the affairs of the nation. But, sadly, the recent generations of our Royal Family have had a poor record as patrons of the arts and sciences. As yet there is little to suggest that the Prince is an exception in that respect. As a man with strong views about architecture, a high public profile and enormous private wealth, he has an extraordinary opportunity to commission buildings for his large estates. But he has yet to produce a noteworthy construction. Where are the commissions to compare with Inigo Jones' Queens' House for James I, Nash's Royal Pavilion for the Prince Regent or the Crystal Palace for Prince Albert? Neither have the Prince's broadcasts and speeches been notable for their scholarly depth. Any number of increasingly facile barbs in the 'carbuncle' mould can not make up for an in-depth and historical examination of the choices facing architects and the public.

In fact the real sadness is that public discussion of architecture has been dominated by invective and vilification rather than informed debate. The Prince of Wales is not the only one to blame in this instance; architectural journalists and critics have generally been very irresponsible in their presentation of the issues. There has been no attempt to bring to light the exhilarating breadth and vitality of the early Modern movements, not to suggest why generations of highly educated architects should identify with its aspirations. Although 'brutalism' and 'the International Style' have received an extensive if malignant press, the 19th-century steel pioneers , Constructivism, Expressionism, Futurism, Naturalism, Plasticism, Rationalism, all might as well never have existed, for all we hear about them from most of out architectural commentators, whether royal or otherwise. No one is willing to object when the Prince treats the Bullring in Birmingham as if it was the very apogee of Modern architecture.

Is an architectural style responsible for the disfigurement of our environment? This is the real question, and if the opponents of Modernism could stop their campaign of vilification for long enough to pose it to themselves they would realise how implausible their position is. The conservationists are right; much that has been built in Britain since the war is quite appalling, and the centres of many of our principle cities have been destroyed. But it is quite unjust to make the 'Modern Movement', or any other movement for that matter, the scapegoat for this.

For as long as we continue to treat the construction of a building as solely an economic venture, our cities, towns and villages will become less and less attractive places to live in. Whether they are dressed in vernacular, Classical or International Style is quite beside the point.

Of course architects have played their part in this debacle. They have been only too willing to concur with their clients, whether developers or public authorities, in the view that their job is to produce a commodity – architecture – which has no bearing on the public at large. But while not wishing to exonerate the architects who have designed the cheap, shoddy developments, I take the view that blaming them alone obscures the extent to which the large corporations, developers and governments are deeply implicated. If a quick profit is the only consideration, then the most valuable architect is one who can get round the planning system, build faster and use the cheapest materials. So it is hardly surprising that buildings reflect the narrow interests of the market place rather than the long term needs of the community.

In particular, the responsibility of government should not be underestimated. The Thatcher years have reminded us, if we needed reminding, of the power of government to effect change where there is a will to do so. Certainly this government has the authority to make it plain, through direct patronage, legislation and incentive taxation, that the shoddy commercial developments of the past will no longer be brooked.

President Mitterrand has much to teach us in this respect. Here is a man who has been democratically elected and who has committed himself not to the rhetoric but to the practicalities of promoting higher architectural standards.

By staging a large number of competitions for young and experienced architects alike, by setting aside funds for big public projects and by encouraging and sometimes compelling public authorities and private companies to stop using routine developers' architects, the French government has radically improved the quality of the nation's architecture, promoting a new generation of talented designers. The fruits of this policy are there to be seen, not only in the splendid 'grand projets' going up all over Paris like the Louvre Pyramid, but also in other remarkable constructions appearing throughout France.

Our cities are in crisis. These once great centres of civic life have become urban jungles where the profiteer and the vehicle rule. Lack of foresight and private greed have eroded this once public realm. There is apparently no modern equivalent to the sense of patronage which engendered the great parks, the market places, the fountains and the majestic tree-lined avenues of the Georgian epoch. John Nash's Regent's Park is in one respect nothing but an enormous developer's housing estate. But it is also a progressive, daring and, of course, beautiful piece of urban planning. Its realisation required determination and vision. Today the little planning that does go on is administered by bureaucratic planning authorities; a negative force with extensive powers of refusal and delay, but entirely lacking the will or the resources to take creative steps to improve the dire condition of our environment.

Britain is uniquely deprived in this respect. On the Continent improvements which repair and enrich the fabric of its cities are in progress everywhere. Municipal governments from Helsinki to Naples are excluding traffic from their city centres, at least at peak times. Meanwhile, the famous agoras of London, the 'people's places', such as Trafalgar Square, Picadilly Circus, Oxford Circus, Marble Arch, Hyde Park Corner and Parliament Square, are becoming ever more dangerous and congested roundabouts. Planning needs vision and large-scale co-ordination; at the very least public authorities must be willing to insert demanding environmental standards into the planning laws, making balconies, parks and cultural amenities as obligatory as fire escapes. Until governments become seriously involved in giving direction, a polluting commercialism will rule and ruin our cities.

Before we can hope to overcome the ugly legacy of the last decades we must recognise both the fragile beauty of the universe and the enormity of the environmental crisis which is threatening mankind. We delude ourselves if we think that returning to a make-believe past can solve this crisis. In fact, the danger we face is not being too modern but rather not being modern enough. In architecture as elsewhere, it is only through the development of the most modern ideas and techniques that we can solve the problems that confront us. We have made great progress in both science and art. As a result, for the first time, we have power to transform our society . But only with an equal advance in ethics, rendering our public life our first concern, can we make our world a more beautiful and humane place to live in.

---

*

SIMON JENKINS
Such an onslaught, but the Prince is right

Simon Jenkins is deputy chairman of English Heritage and a regular contributor to The Sunday Times, *where this article first appeared. Written in response to Rogers' outspoken critique of the Prince, Jenkins here pinpoints the weaknesses in his argument.*

Goodness, British architecture is hotting up. Nor could it ask for a more torrid row than between that evergreen fogey, Prince Charles, and the bedenimed survivor of the old Modernism, Richard Rogers. But what got into Rogers in *The Times*?

No cliché is left unturned. The work of his contemporaries is still 'pastiche Disneyland'. Nostalgia is still rose-tinted. Cities are still in crisis. Society is still to blame. The prince is secretive and undemocratic.

By my count, Rogers scores just a couple of royal flesh wounds. Certainly the Prince needs to be careful when he intrudes his emphatic views into the planning process, and perhaps he should attend at least one of the stiflingly tedious debates which architects hold to discuss his views.

But Rogers is grossly unfair in accusing him of neglecting his power of patronage. Last month, the Prince revealed Leon Krier's proposal for a new town on the Duchy of Cornwall estate in Dorchester. It offers a style and humanity not seen in British town planning this century. Rogers clearly dislikes Krier, an enthusiast for medieval and Renaissance town layouts. But Krier has a finger on the pulse of the future and a courageous royal patron to boot.

Rogers goes on to confuse two wholly different definitions of Modernism. He himself is a stern apostle of the Modern Movement, whose dwindling adherents gather still round the guttering flame of Le Corbusier and Mies van der Rohe: less is more, ornament is weakness, architecture is social engineering, new is great. Rogers may deplore nostalgia, but few stylistic schools are so long in the tooth and bedecked with cobwebs as this one. Modernism is entitled to the affection of conservationists, but the style proved horribly susceptible to debasement, and yielded some of Britain's ugliest and most unpopular city developments.

When Rogers implicitly equates them to Wren's St Paul's and the great Gothic cathedrals one is tempted simply to say with Dr Johnson, No Sir! and walk away. The Birmingham Bullring and the Elephant and Castle were not minor aberrations from a great style. They were the appallingly visible betrayal of a once humanist profession, under the influence of an illiberal dogma. A more sensitive calling would condemn them outright rather them find weasel words to excuse them. Prince Charles struck a deep popular chord in his attack on these buildings. The attack loses none of its force for his not being elected. Since when were those who prick the professions expected to force the voters?

But Modernism has less and less to do with modern architecture. By lumping together his favourite style with all 'modern architecture', Rogers seeks to tar critics of the former with being opposed to all novelty and change. This gambit is naive.

In his famous television programme, Prince Charles praised a bevy of modern architects and buildings: Michael Hopkins, Terry Farrell, Quinlan Terry, Jeremy Dixon, the Lord's grandstand, Covent Garden, Richmond riverside, new hospitals, community housing projects, dock restorations.

Rogers may vilify them. He attacks Robert Venturi's National Gallery extension as pastiche. He ridicules as a 'stage set' Julian Bicknell's Moscow embassy residence. He dismisses all revivalism as a 'collage of disposable symbols . . . this Disneyland approach'.

I suppose the same could be said to Robert Smythson and the Baroque of Vanbrugh and Hawksmoor. The abuse of past architectural styles – often in the cause of demolishing old buildings standing in the way of development – comes strange from those trapped in the fusty intellectual cell of Corbusian dogmatism.

The most exiting feature of modern British architecture, properly so-called, is that it is breaking free of this dogmatism. There is a new affection for colour, for stone, marble and brick, for ornament and decoration, for delicacy in detail, for the artifice, illusion and humour that was a feature of British architecture from Inigo Jones to Lutyens. Certainly solecisms have been committed in the name of this freedom but architecture is not served by vilifying the freedom itself.

Modernism fed on reaction against the often barren revivalism of the Edwardians. The popularity of today's Post-Modernism, the crowds flocking to Quinlan Terry's Neo-Classical Richmond river bank and to the warm eclecticism of Covent Garden, is likewise a reaction against the Modernist minimalism. We are small of mind when we fail to appreciate the continuity of this cultural cycle.

Rogers has outspokenly supported the demolition of a building by that vigorous Edwardian John Belcher, to make way for the Palumbo block next to the Mansion House. 'Rose-tinted nostalgia', he says of Belcher's defenders. Yet architects are unique among artists in demanding the right to destroy the work of others to make way for their own creations. Dead architects may have no rights, but those of us who enjoy their work and find it a comfort and a joy in turbulent times surely do.

To plead for the continued presence around us of old buildings, and to enjoy new ones that respect that continuity, is not perverse. Only those lacking in self-confidence want to obliterate the past, as if frightened of the comparison. Rogers himself pleads that his buildings are 'contextual', but the context is that supplied by conservation. Where would I M Pei's Paris pyramid be without the Louvre, or Wright's Guggenheim without old Fifth Avenue? Rogers' Lloyd's building derives its appeal from the juxtaposition with the (saved) Leadenhall Market.

This context – the roughly two per cent of English buildings enjoying hesitant statutory protection – is under constant threat from pressures to which too many architects in the past lent avid support. Rogers excuses the excesses of architecture on the alarming grounds that his profession 'mirrors society, its civility and its barbarism'. Full marks at least for frankness. But those who struggle to resist the barbaric in architecture must seek what allies they can. Thank goodness for the Prince.

NEW TOWN ORDINANCES & CODES
Andres Duany, Elizabeth Plater-Zyberk, Chester E Chellman

VIEW OF SEASIDE, MIAMI, FLORIDA, 1987

The composition of building codes has become the trade-mark of architects Andres Duany and Elizabeth Plater-Zyberk, whose influential development at Seaside, Florida, was conceived in response to the decaying centres of American cities. By establishing a basic set of rules, reproduced here with the code for Seaside, they enable the participation of a wide variety of architects, while maintaining the essential character of the urban environment.

The congested, fragmented, unsatisfying suburbs and the disintegrating urban centres of today are not the products of *laissez-faire*, nor are they the inevitable results of mindless greed. They are thoroughly planned to be as they are: the direct result of zoning and subdivision ordinances zealously administered by thousands of planning departments.

America since the war is the result of these ordinances – 'conventional' lot subdivisions in the 40s and 50s and Planned Unit Developments (PUDs) since. If the results are dismaying, it is because the current model of the city being projected is dismal. Today's ordinances dictate only four criteria for urbanism: the free and rapid flow of traffic; parking in quantity; the rigorous separation of uses; and a relatively low density of building. The latter two demand an amorphic waste of land, and car traffic has become the central, unavoidable experience of the public realm.

The traditional pattern of walkable, mixed-use neighbourhoods is not encouraged and, more often than not, inadvertently proscribed by some provisions of these ordinances. Designers find themselves in the ironic situation of being forbidden from building in the manner of our most admired historic places. One cannot propose a new Charleston or New Orleans without seeking substantial variances from current codes.

There are over 38,000 municipalities in the United States. Most of them are projecting their growth on the basis of ordinances which are virtual recipes for urban disintegration. There are not the means, nor is there time, to educate the hundreds of thousands of planners and administrators who are now active, of the needed changes. There is, however, a mechanism in place to effect the change efficiently; that is to change the ordinances themselves. Planners are not prepared to be re-educated, but they are accustomed to following the law. It is thus possible, by modifying these codes, to prescribe a more workable and rational urbanism. The Traditional Neighbourhood Development Ordinance (TND) is such an ordinance.

The TND Ordinance is a declaration for new neighbourhood planning to be guided by the sensible and desirable attributes of traditional neighbourhoods. The TND Ordinance promotes independence from the automobile by bringing the needs of daily living within walking distance of the residence. By reducing the number of automobile trips and the length of those trips, certain social objectives are achieved; increased personal time, reduced traffic congestion, and conservation of land and fuel. The TND Ordinance promotes security through neighbourliness. By walking instead of driving, citizens come to know each other and the bonds of an authentic community are established. The TND Ordinance promotes social integration of age and economic classes by providing a full range of housing types and commercial opportunities. Finally, the TND Ordinance promotes the democratic initiatives of education, recreation, health maintenance, child care, and public assembly by providing incentives for civic facilities.

T.N.D. ORDINANCE
TRADITIONAL NEIGHBORHOOD DEVELOPMENT

1. INTENT

This ordinance is designed to ensure the development of open land along the lines of traditional neighborhoods. Its provisions adopt the urban conventions which were normal in the United States from colonial times until the 1940's.

Traditional neighborhoods share the following conventions:

- Dwellings, shops and workplaces, all limited in size, are located in close proximity to each other.

- A variety of streets serve equitably the needs of the pedestrian and the automobile.

- Well-defined squares and parks provide places for informal social activity and recreation.

- Well-placed civic buildings provide places of purposeful assembly for social, cultural and religious activities, becoming symbols of community identity.

- Private buildings are located along streets and squares forming a disciplined edge unbroken by parking lots.

Traditional neighborhoods achieve certain social objectives:

- By reducing the number and length of necessary automobile trips, traffic congestion is minimized and commuters are granted increased personal time.

- By bringing most of the needs of daily living within walking distance, the elderly and the young gain independence of movement.

- By walking in defined public spaces, citizens come to know each other and to watch over their collective security.

- By providing a full range of housing types and workplaces, age and economic class are integrated and the bonds of an authentic community are formed.

- By promoting suitable civic buildings, democratic initiatives are encouraged and the organic evolution of the society is secured.

Until the advent of postwar zoning ordinances, traditional neighborhoods were commonplace in the United States. Many survive as examples of communities which continue to be practical and desirable today.

This document developed in part with a grant from the National Endowment for the Arts.

DRAFT   FEBRUARY 15, 1989

© Foundation for Traditional Neighborhoods
Post Office Box 440
Ossippee, New Hampshire 03864

2. LAND USE

GENERAL

2.1 The TND Option shall constitute an overlay district available by right where current zoning allows any use except industrial.

2.2 The TND Option requires a minimum contiguous parcel of 40 acres and a maximum of 200 acres. Larger parcels shall be developed as multiples, individually subject to the TND provisions below.

2.3 The Developer of the TND shall demonstrate the availability and adequacy of access roads and utilities.

PUBLIC

2.4 Public Tracts contain publicly owned Parks, Squares, Greenbelts, streets and alleys.

CIVIC

2.5 Civic Lots contain publicly or privately owned buildings of communal use such as Neighborhood Halls, libraries, post offices, schools, day care centers, clubhouses, religious buildings, recreational facilities and the like.

SHOPFRONT

2.6 Shopfront Lots contain privately owned buildings for retail, restaurant, office, entertainment, Lodging, Artisanal and residential uses.

2.7 No less than 25 % of the building area must be maintained for residential use.

ROWHOUSE

2.8 Rowhouse Lots contain privately owned buildings for residential, Limited Office, and Limited Lodging uses.

HOUSE

2.9 House Lots contain privately owned buildings for residential, Limited Office, and Limited Lodging uses.

WORKSHOP

2.10 Workshop Lots contain privately owned buildings for Automotive and Light Manufacturing.

3. LAND ALLOCATION

GENERAL

3.1 The entire land area of a TND shall be subdivided into Public Tracts and Lots.

3.2 Similar Lot types shall generally enfront acros Street Tracts. Dissimilar Lot types may enfront acros Square and Park Tracts or abut at rear lot lines.

PUBLIC

3.3 A minimum of 15% of the land area of a TND shall be permanently allocated to Park or Square Tracts.

3.4 Natural vistas such as waterfronts and promontories shall have 50% of their perimeter allocated Street Tracts.

3.5 Golf courses shall be located within Greenbelt Tracts.

CIVIC

3.6 A minimum of 5% of the land area of a TND shall be dedicated to Civic Lots.

3.7 Civic Lots shall be located within or adjacent Square or Park Tracts or on a Street Vista.

3.8 The Developer shall covenant to construct Neighborhood Hall on a Civic Lot upon the sale 75% of the lots.

3.9 The construction of buildings on Civic Lots shall be supported by an ongoing assessment through Homeowners' Association.

3.10 For each increment of 50 dwellings, there shall be a Civic Lot of 5000 sq. ft. reserved for day-care use and dedicated to public ownership.

SHOPFRONT

3.11 A minimum of 5% and a maximum of 50% of total land area of a TND shall be permanently dedicated to Shopfront Lots.

ROWHOUSE

3.12 A maximum of 8 Rowhouse lots may be consolidated for the purpose of constructing a single apartment building containing dwellings equal number to the lots consolidated.

3.13 Setbacks on consolidated Rowhouse shall apply as in a single lot.

HOUSE

3.14 A maximum of three House Lots may be consolidated for the purpose of constructing a single building.

3.15 Setbacks on consolidated House Lots shall apply as in a single lot.

WORKSHOP

3.16 A minimum of 5% and a maximum of 25% of the total land area of a TND shall be permanently dedicated to Workshop Lots.

4. LOTS BUILDINGS	5. STREETS ALLEYS	6. PARKING	7. DEFINITIONS
...ots shall share a Frontage Line no less than ...g with a Street or Park Tract. ...ildings shall have their main entrance open-...reet or Park Tract. ...s, open colonnades and open porches may ...up to 10 ft. into the front setbacks. ...ns of buildings having a footprint of not ...150 sq. ft. shall be exempted from height ...s. ...ng walls placed less than 5 feet from a side ...: line shall remain windowless and doors ...re rated.	5.1 Streets shall provide access to all Public Tracts and Private Lots. 5.2 All streets shall terminate at other streets within the TND and connect to existing and projected streets outside the TND. 5.3 The average perimeter of all Blocks within the TND shall not exceed 2000 ft. 5.4 Utilities shall run along Alley Tracts wherever possible. 5.5 Streetlamps shall be installed on both sides of Street Tracts at no more than 75 ft. intervals measured diagonally across the streets. 5.6 Streetrees shall be installed on both sides of Street Tracts at no more than 75 ft. intervals measured diagonally across the street.	6.1 On-street parking directly enfronting a lot shall count toward fulfilling the parking requirement of that lot. 6.2 Parking lots shall generally be located at the rear or at the side of buildings and shall be screened from the sidewalk by Streetwalls. 6.3 Parking lots and parking garages shall not be located at street intersections. 6.4 Adjacent parking lots shall have internal vehicular connections. 6.5 Parking lots shall be landscaped with one Shade Tree per six parking spaces.	Terms in general use throughout this ordinance shall take their common accepted meaning. Terms requiring interpretation specific to this ordinance are defined as follows: **Artisanal Use:** Premises for the manufacture and sale of artifacts employing only handwork and/or table mounted electrical machinery emitting no odors or noise beyond the immediate premises. **Attic:** The habitable area within the pitch of a roof. **Automotive Use:** Premises for the selling, servicing and/or repairing of motorized wheeled vehicles.
...aies and open colonnades shall be permitted ...ch up to 10 ft. into a Public Tract. Such ...ments shall be protected by easements.	5.7 Public Tracts containing Squares shall provide a street along their perimeter which conforms to the specifications corresponding to the efronting lot types. 5.8 Streets forming part of the State highway systems shall conform to State highway standards.	6.6 The Developer shall demonstrate the provision of adequate parking for Public Tracts containing Squares and Parks. 6.7 Parking lots on Public Tracts, shall be graded, compacted and landscaped, but may be left unpaved.	**Block:** The aggregate of lots and Alley Tracts circumscribed by a continuous set of Street Tracts **Curb Radius:** The curved edge of the street at an intersection measured at the inner edge of the parking lane. **Facade:** The wall of a building which corresponds to a lot Frontage **Frontage Line:** The lot line which coincides with a Street Tract.
...ngs located on Civic Lots shall be subject ...nt or setback limitations. ...ngs located on Civic Lots shall be painted ...t color throughout the TND.	5.9 Civic lots shall enfront on tracts containing streets which conform to the street specifications of the adjacent Lot Types.	6.8 The Developer shall demonstrate the provision of adequate parking for the various types of Civic buildings. Shared parking shall be permitted where day/night and workday/holiday schedules do not overlap (i.e. Neighborhood Halls). 6.9 Parking lots for Civic buildings used principally on holidays must be graded, compacted and planted, but may be left unpaved (i.e. religious buildings). 6.10 No less than 75 % of the off-street parking places shall be to the rear of the building. Access may be through the Frontage.	**Greenbelt:** An open area surrounding the built-up area of a TND along 75% of its perimeter; being no less than 50% of the total area of the TND and no less than 200 ft. wide at any place. The area shall be preserved in perpetuity in its natural condition, or used for farming, animal husbandry, golf courses, or subdivided into House lots no smaller than 5 acres. **Homeowner's Association:** The owners of lots and buildings within the TND, incorporated under the auspices of articles which safeguard the rights of the owners in compliance with the laws of the State. The document shall institute a system or representative government by the assembly of the owners maintaining prerogatives for the developer greater than that of the owners only during the period of sales. The document shall set: standards for construction and maintenance on private lots; provisions for maintenance on public tracts; and support for the construction of new buildings on civic lots by an ongoing special assessment equivalent to no less than 10% of the total yearly assessment of the Association. **Light Manufacturing Use:** Buildings for the repair, assembly or fabrication of artifacts emitting no atmospheric pollution, no noxious smells beyond the lot lines and noise for a period no longer than 8 daytime hours. **Limited Lodging Use:** Buildings providing no more than 8 rooms for short-term letting and food service before noon only.
...ngs on Shopfront Lots shall have the Facade ...dy on the Frontage Line along 60% of its ...lings on Shopfront Lots shall have no re-...acks from the side lot lines. ...ings on Shopfront Lots shall cover no more ...f the lot area. ...ings on Shopfront Lots shall not exceed 4 ...eight.	5.10 Shopfront Lots shall enfront on Tracts containing streets consisting of two 12 ft. travel lanes, one 10 ft. central turning lane and diagonal parking on both sides. Sidewalks shall be no less than 12 ft. wide and the Curb Radius shall not exceed 15 ft. 5.11 Shopfront Lots shall have their rear lot lines coinciding with an alley tract 24 ft. wide containing a vehicular pavement width of 8 ft.	6.11 There shall be one parking space per 250 sq. ft. of building available for restaurant, office, entertainment and artisanal uses; one per room of lodging and one per two bedrooms of residential use. 6.12 No less than 75 % of the parking places shall be to the rear of the building. Access may be through the Frontage.	**Limited Office Use:** Buildings for the transaction of business or the supply of professional services, employing no more than 8 persons. **Lodging Use:** Buildings providing food service and rooms for short-term letting **Neighborhood Hall:** A public assembly building containing at least one room having an area equivalent to 20 sq. ft. per dwelling. **Neighborhood Proper:** The built-up area of a TND, including lots, Parks and Squares but excluding Greenbelt areas. **Park:** An open space, paved no more than 10% of its area, naturalistically landscaped, and surrounded by building lots on 75% of its perimeter.
...ngs on Rowhouse Lots shall be setback ...and 15 ft. from the Frontage Line. Build-...et intersections must be setback 5 ft. from ...age Lines. ...ings on Rowhouse Lots shall have no re-...acks from the side lot lines. ...ngs on Rowhouse Lots shall cover no more ...f the lot area. ...ings on Rowhouse Lots shall not exceed 3 ...s Raised Basement in height.	5.12 Rowhouse Lots shall enfront on Tracts containing streets consisting of two 11 ft. travel lanes and parallel parking on both sides. Sidewalks shall be no less than 6 ft. wide and the Curb Radius shall not exceed 15 ft. 5.13 Rowhouse Lots shall have their rear lot lines coinciding with an alley tract 24 ft. wide containing a vehicular pavement width of 8 ft.	6.13 There shall be one parking place per 250 sq. ft. of office, one per room of lodging and one per two bedrooms of residential use. 6.14 All off-street parking places shall be to the rear of the building. Access shall be through a vehicular alley only.	**Raised Basement:** A semi-underground story serving to raise the principal floor level no more than 5 ft. above the sidewalk. **Shade Tree:** A deciduous tree of wide canopy, resistant to root pressure and sodium, no less than 4" caliper and 8 ft. clear trunk at the time of planting. **Square:** An open space paved not less than 35% of its area surrounded by building lots on 90% of its perimeter. **Streetwall:** A masonry wall or wood fence built along the Frontage Line between 3 and 8 ft. in height.
...ings on House Lots shall be setback be-...nd 35 ft. from the Frontage Line. ...ings on House Lots shall be setback from ...lines equivalent to no less than 20% of the ...e lot. The entire setback may be allocated ... ...ings on House Lots shall be setback no less ... from the rear lot line. ...ings on House Lots shall cover no more ...f the lot area. ...ings on House Lots shall not exceed 2 ...s Attic in height. ...ings on House Lots with front setbacks ...20 ft. shall have a Streetwall built along ...Frontage Line.	5.14 House Lots shall enfront on tracts containing streets consisting of two 10 ft. travel lanes and parallel parking on one side. Sidewalks shall be no less than 4 ft. wide and the Curb Radius shall not exceed 25 ft. 5.15 House Lots shall have their rear lot lines coinciding with an alley tract 10 ft. wide containing a pedestrian pavement width of 4 ft.	6.15 There shall be one parking place per 250 sq. ft. of office, per room of lodging and one per two bedrooms of residential use. 6.16 All off-street parking places shall be to the side or the rear of the building. Garages or carports shall be located a minimum of 20 feet behind the Facade. Access may be through the Frontage.	**Story:** a habitable level within a building no more than 14 ft. in height from finished floor to finished ceiling. **Street Lamps:** A light standard between 8 and 14 ft. in height equipped with an incandescent or metal halide light source. **Street Tree:** A deciduous tree or palm resistant to root pressure and sodium, no less than 4 in caliper and 8 ft. clear trunk at the time of planting. **Street Vista:** A building site located to terminate the view down the axis of a Street Tract.
...ings on Workshop Lots shall not require ...om any lot line. ...ings on Workshop Lots shall cover no more ...f the lot area. ...ings on Workshop Lots shall not exceed 2 ...eight. ...shop Lots shall be separated from other lot ...e side and rear lot lines by a continuous ...all no less than 10 ft. in height.	5.16 Workshop Lots shall enfront on streets containing streets consisting of two 10 ft. central turning lane and parallel parking on both sides. Sidewalks shall be no less than 4 ft. wide and the Curb Radius shall not exceed 35 ft. 5.17 Workshop Lots shall have their rear lot lines coinciding with an alley tract 24 ft. wide containing a vehicular pavement width of 8 ft.	6.17 There shall be one parking place per 250 sq. ft. of building. 6.18 Off-street parking places may be to the front, the side or the rear of the building.	

...UP BY ANDRES DUANY, ELIZABETH PLATER-ZYBERK & CHESTER E CHELLMAN

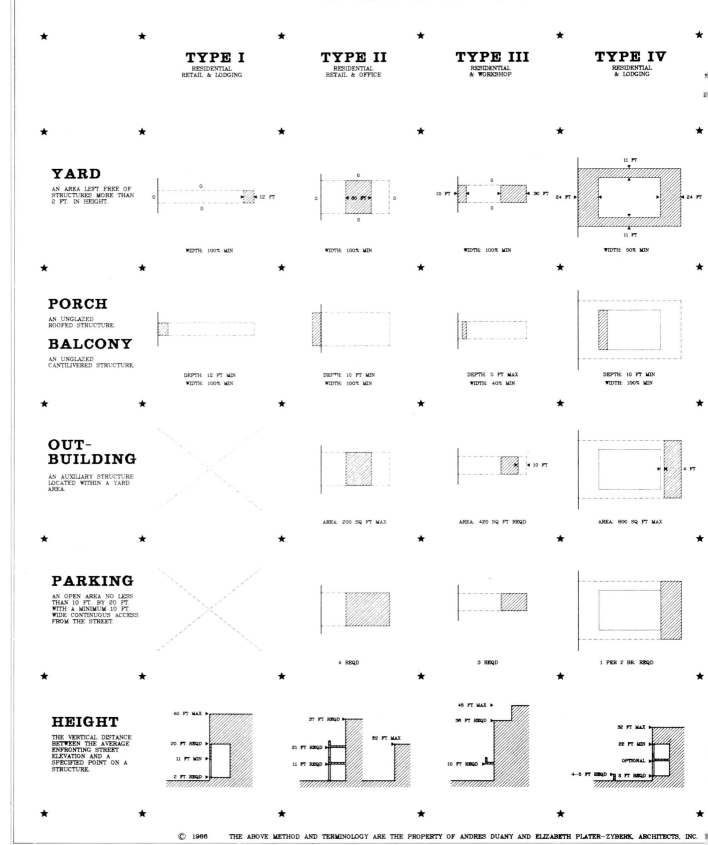

TYPE I
RESIDENTIAL
RETAIL & LODGING

TYPE II
RESIDENTIAL
RETAIL & OFFICE

TYPE III
RESIDENTIAL
& WORKSHOP

TYPE IV
RESIDENTIAL
& LODGING

YARD
AN AREA LEFT FREE OF
STRUCTURES MORE THAN
2 FT. IN HEIGHT.

WIDTH: 100% MIN — WIDTH: 100% MIN — WIDTH: 100% MIN — WIDTH: 50% MIN

PORCH
AN UNGLAZED
ROOFED STRUCTURE.

BALCONY
AN UNGLAZED
CANTILIVERED STRUCTURE.

DEPTH: 12 FT MIN / WIDTH: 100% MIN
DEPTH: 10 FT MIN / WIDTH: 100% MIN
DEPTH: 5 FT MAX / WIDTH: 40% MIN
DEPTH: 10 FT MIN / WIDTH: 100% MIN

OUT-BUILDING
AN AUXILIARY STRUCTURE
LOCATED WITHIN A YARD
AREA.

AREA: 200 SQ FT MAX — AREA: 420 SQ FT REQD — AREA: 800 SQ FT MAX

PARKING
AN OPEN AREA NO LESS
THAN 10 FT. BY 20 FT.
WITH A MINIMUM 10 FT.
WIDE CONTINUOUS ACCESS
FROM THE STREET.

4 REQD — 3 REQD — 1 PER 2 BR. REQD

HEIGHT
THE VERTICAL DISTANCE
BETWEEN THE AVERAGE
ENFRONTING STREET
ELEVATION AND A
SPECIFIED POINT ON A
STRUCTURE.

OWN OF SEASIDE

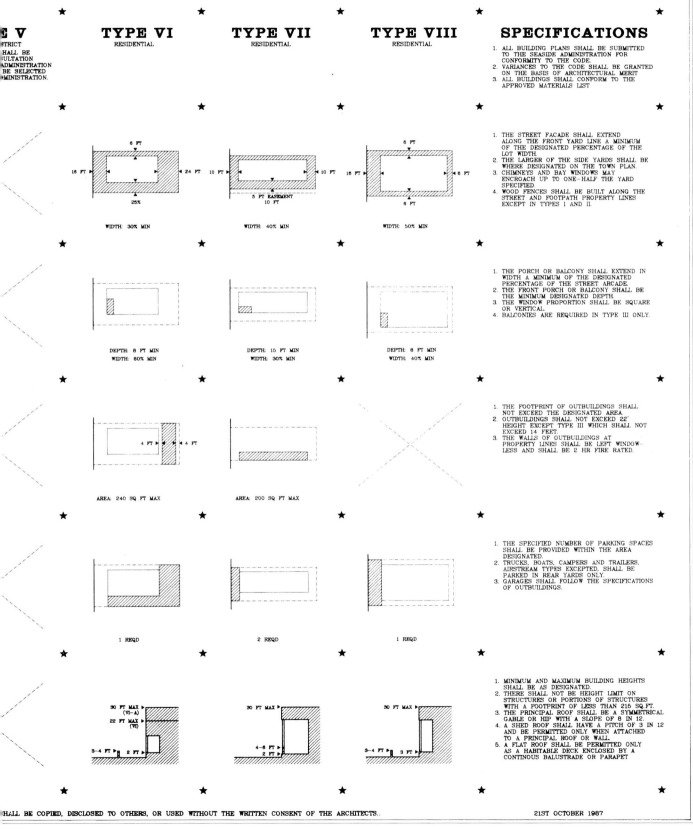

E V	**TYPE VI** RESIDENTIAL	**TYPE VII** RESIDENTIAL	**TYPE VIII** RESIDENTIAL	**SPECIFICATIONS**

E V
TRICT
HALL BE
ULTATION
ADMINISTRATION
BE SELECTED
MINISTRATION.

SPECIFICATIONS

1. ALL BUILDING PLANS SHALL BE SUBMITTED TO THE SEASIDE ADMINISTRATION FOR CONFORMITY TO THE CODE.
2. VARIANCES TO THE CODE SHALL BE GRANTED ON THE BASIS OF ARCHITECTURAL MERIT
3. ALL BUILDINGS SHALL CONFORM TO THE APPROVED MATERIALS LIST

1. THE STREET FACADE SHALL EXTEND ALONG THE FRONT YARD LINE A MINIMUM OF THE DESIGNATED PERCENTAGE OF THE LOT WIDTH.
2. THE LARGER OF THE SIDE YARDS SHALL BE WHERE DESIGNATED ON THE TOWN PLAN.
3. CHIMNEYS AND BAY WINDOWS MAY ENCROACH UP TO ONE-HALF THE YARD SPECIFIED.
4. WOOD FENCES SHALL BE BUILT ALONG THE STREET AND FOOTPATH PROPERTY LINES EXCEPT IN TYPES I AND II.

- TYPE VI: WIDTH: 30% MIN
- TYPE VII: WIDTH: 40% MIN
- TYPE VIII: WIDTH: 50% MIN

1. THE PORCH OR BALCONY SHALL EXTEND IN WIDTH A MINIMUM OF THE DESIGNATED PERCENTAGE OF THE STREET ARCADE.
2. THE FRONT PORCH OR BALCONY SHALL BE THE MINIMUM DESIGNATED DEPTH.
3. THE WINDOW PROPORTION SHALL BE SQUARE OR VERTICAL.
4. BALCONIES ARE REQUIRED IN TYPE III ONLY.

- TYPE VI: DEPTH: 8 FT MIN / WIDTH: 60% MIN
- TYPE VII: DEPTH: 15 FT MIN / WIDTH: 30% MIN
- TYPE VIII: DEPTH: 8 FT MIN / WIDTH: 40% MIN

1. THE FOOTPRINT OF OUTBUILDINGS SHALL NOT EXCEED THE DESIGNATED AREA.
2. OUTBUILDINGS SHALL NOT EXCEED 22' HEIGHT EXCEPT TYPE III WHICH SHALL NOT EXCEED 14 FEET.
3. THE WALLS OF OUTBUILDINGS AT PROPERTY LINES SHALL BE LEFT WINDOW-LESS AND SHALL BE 2 HR FIRE RATED.

- TYPE VI: AREA: 240 SQ FT MAX
- TYPE VII: AREA: 200 SQ FT MAX

1. THE SPECIFIED NUMBER OF PARKING SPACES SHALL BE PROVIDED WITHIN THE AREA DESIGNATED.
2. TRUCKS, BOATS, CAMPERS AND TRAILERS, AIRSTREAM TYPES EXCEPTED, SHALL BE PARKED IN REAR YARDS ONLY.
3. GARAGES SHALL FOLLOW THE SPECIFICATIONS OF OUTBUILDINGS.

- TYPE VI: 1 REQD
- TYPE VII: 2 REQD
- TYPE VIII: 1 REQD

1. MINIMUM AND MAXIMUM BUILDING HEIGHTS SHALL BE AS DESIGNATED.
2. THERE SHALL NOT BE HEIGHT LIMIT ON STRUCTURES OR PORTIONS OF STRUCTURES WITH A FOOTPRINT OF LESS THAN 215 SQ.FT.
3. THE PRINCIPAL ROOF SHALL BE A SYMMETRICAL GABLE OR HIP WITH A SLOPE OF 8 IN 12.
4. A SHED ROOF SHALL HAVE A PITCH OF 3 IN 12 AND BE PERMITTED ONLY WHEN ATTACHED TO A PRINCIPAL ROOF OR WALL.
5. A FLAT ROOF SHALL BE PERMITTED ONLY AS A HABITABLE DECK ENCLOSED BY A CONTINOUS BALUSTRADE OR PARAPET

21ST OCTOBER 1987

SEASIDE, MIAMI, FLORIDA, 1987

VIEW OF HALL FROM LANDING

DEMETRI PORPHYRIOS
House in Kensington, 1987

VIEW OF HALL

This new five-storey family house in a residential area of Kensington replaces the existing dilapidated building. It is in a terrace that dates from the late 18th and early 19th centuries, well maintained with the occasional extension or refurbishment. The overall character of the street is Neo-Classical.

The site is rather restricted by a frontage of only nine metres. We decided to keep the planimetric organisation typical of such houses. Laterally, the building is organised in two unequal bays, a sensible and time-honoured solution, since by grouping circulation and ancillary spaces along the narrow bay, the rest of the frontage is freed for reception rooms.

Traditionally, the staircase connects all the floors, not making a distinction between the public reception areas and the private bedrooms. But here, because of

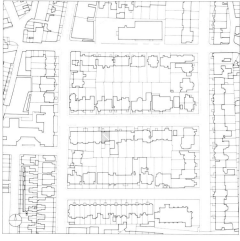

SITE PLAN

the size of the house, we felt it necessary to distinguish. This we achieved by differentiating both spatially and figuratively between the entrance hall staircase and the everyday oval staircase next to the lift.

The entrance hall staircase has its own room, seven metres high, connecting the library and dining-room with the first-floor reception rooms. At ground floor the library connects with the dining-room, which opens onto a terrace overlooking the garden. Guests have direct access to the conservatory by means of the oval staircase. At garden level are the family room, kitchen and all ancillary and service spaces. The master bedroom suite occupies most of the first floor, with bedroom, dressing room and bathroom organised in enfilade fashion revealing the full depth of the house, avoiding any axial emphasis.

The first floor is devoted entirely to the

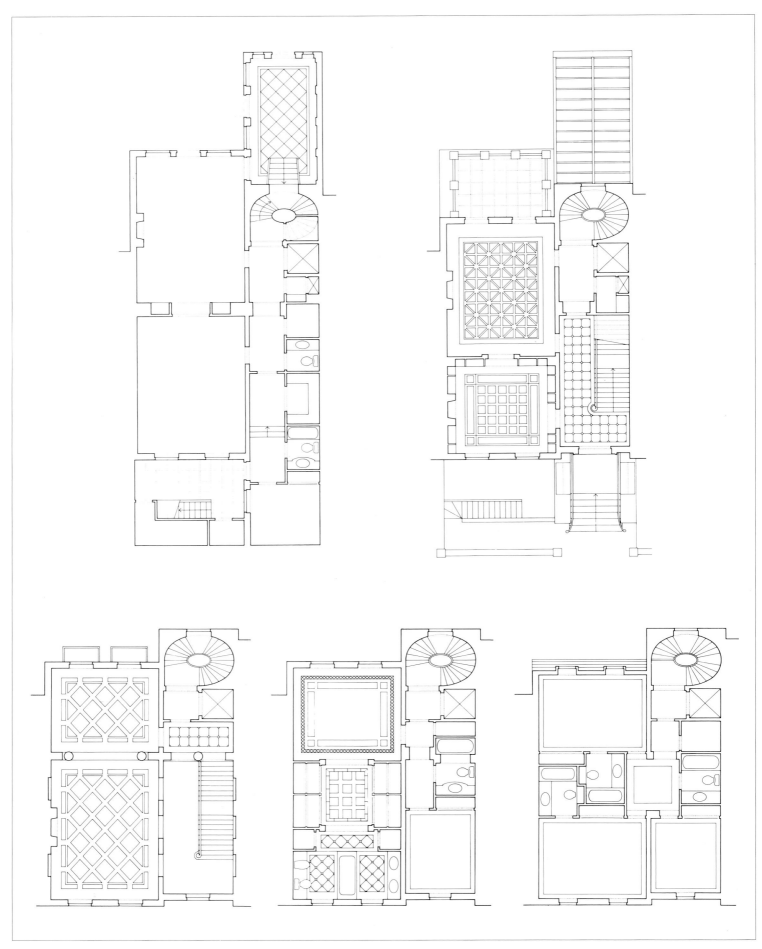

ABOVE L TO R: BASEMENT AND GROUND-FLOOR PLANS; *BELOW L TO R*: FIRST-, SECOND- AND THIRD-FLOOR PLANS

STREET ELEVATION

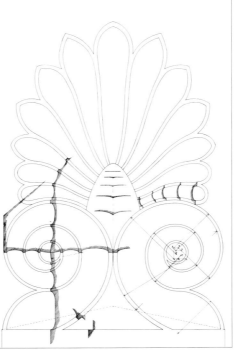

drawing room. This connects visually with the double-space entrance hall through three internal windows. The full extent of the house is revealed, with floor to ceiling height measuring almost four metres.

The tripartite articulation of the street elevation into rusticated base, *piano nobile* and attic top is marked by the cornice that crowns the *piano nobile* and drawing room and the entrance hall window architraves.

The tower of the oval staircase, the conservatory and the family room project from the main volume of the house at the rear. The pilasters and glazed intercolumniations at garden level act as a base on top of which the house rises in three stages, crowned by a steep slated roof.

Externally the street elevation is rendered and painted off-white, while the rear elevation is faced in brick, except for the rendered garden-level extension. The front steps are stone and all profiles to cornices, window architraves, diestones

ABOVE: VIEW OF LIBRARY; *BELOW L TO R*: VIEW OF CONSERVATORY; DETAIL OF ANTHEMION

and the pedimented front entrance were rendered *in situ*.

Internal walls are plastered and painted or finished in stretched fabric. The entrance hall has a stucco base divided into painted panels with ocre paint above. Reception room floors are parquet, bedrooms carpeted, bathrooms and conservatory marble and the entrance hall stone.

All internal cornices, coffers and anathemia to pediments have profiles in fibrous plaster. The Doric columns are plaster of Paris. All joinery is custom-made in hardwood for painting. The panelling and bookcases for the library are in English oak stained and polished. We also designed light fittings for the entrance hall and all metalwork for railings internally and externally.

Project Team: Demetri Porphyrios, Alireza Sagharchi, Ian Sutherland, Liam O'Connor, Nigel Cox; *Structural Engineers*: Cameron Taylor Partners; *Client*: Balli Developments Ltd.

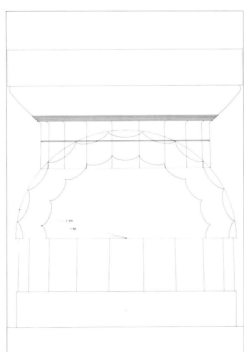

ABOVE: DRAWING ROOM AND HALL; *BELOW L TO R*: DETAIL OF DORIC COLUMN; VIEW OF DRAWING ROOM

F. FANTOZZI. *GEOMETRIC PLAN OF FLORENCE*. 1843

FLORENTINE NEW TOWNS
David Friedman

GIORGIO VASARI AND GIOVANNI STRADANO, *ALLEGORY OF SAN GIOVANNI VALDARNO*, DETAIL, 1563-65

It is perhaps a fortuitous coincidence that the publication of this book, concentrating as it does on the concept of of new towns founded on symmetry and centrality, unified by a system of public squares, streets and monuments, should come at a time when public attention has been focused by the Prince on the disintegration of modern cities, and the idea of medieval town planning as representing the perfect model for contemporary urban design.

The subject of this book is a group of five towns founded by the city of Florence between 1299 and 1350. San Giovanni is one of them; the others are Castelfranco di Sopra, Terranuova, Scarperia, and Firenzuola. The documentation for the unrealised plan for Giglio Fiorentino adds further information. The towns preserve their medieval plans relatively well. In the best of them there is a grandness of conception and an attention to detail that raises orthogonal planning to the level of art.

In the Florentine new towns the discipline of straight lines and right angles is rigorously enforced; it is, however, only the medium for expressing more sophisticated formal ideas. Symmetry dominates the plans. The main street is one axis of composition; a line drawn perpendicular to it, through the middle of a central square, is a second. A large number of parts of the plans conform to the magnetic field of these lines, from the arrangement of building lots around the square to the configuration of the town's defenses. The variety of size and shape of the elements integrated into San Giovanni's orthogonal matrix is extraordinary. Long blocks oriented parallel to the axis of the main street are made to fit comfortably with a square of extended proportions perpendicular to them. In contrast to the mechanical repetition of like units that is sometimes held up as the paradigm of medieval new-town planning, the complexity of Florentine designs distinguishes them as the most accomplished urban projects of their age.

The Florentine new towns were works of art in the literal sense that their designers were artists. We do not know this about any other medieval new-town project. In part this is the result of the

surviving documentation. For most new towns only the official acts of foundation are preserved. These documents assign authority and grant legal privilege; they say almost nothing about design and construction. The Florentine archives preserve both this and another level of record; in addition to legislative documents, the deliberations and financial accounts of planning committees and builders chronicle the city's activities as a founder of towns. The daily records identify the designers of the new towns as mason-architects from the circle of builders active in the city's public projects. Careful examination of the plans reveals their contribution. In an age in which geometry was considered the essence of art, the indispensable theoretical base for all design, the geometrically generated proportions of the new-town plans are a sure sign of the participation of professionals in the design process.

The new towns were built to serve Florence. They were fortresses in newly acquired territory, markets that collected produce for the city, and centres of loyal population. They became administrative capitals of the expanded Florentine state and the main resting places on routes that brought people and merchandise from all over Europe. The towns represented Florence, both to its new subjects and to travellers; their very names proclaimed their allegiance to the city. San Giovanni was the name of the city's patron saint; Firenzuola and Giglio Fiorentino borrowed Florence's own name. The towns tied the land to the capital by presenting models of urban life to the rural population. The public institutions of the new towns were copies of Florentine examples. Through them the residents of the settlements assimilated city ways and integrated themselves into the life of the state. By the 15th century men from the new towns were making important contributions to events within the city.

The Florence that the new towns represented was itself a recent creation. A merchant regime came to power in the city in 1282 with the expansion of public authority as one of its principal goals. This political idea had many implications for the physical character of the city. The government took control of the urban environment in a way that no previous regime had. It passed the first law of eminent domain since antiquity and embarked on an ambitious programme of reconstruction and expansion. The new cathedral, the monumental town hall, numerous churches, and the circuit of walls that increased the size of the city five-fold were all projects undertaken by the merchant commune.

The plan of the city underwent a major transformation in this period. From a townscape of isolated neighbourhoods shot through with back alleys accessible only to the people who inhabited them and dominated by the urban castles of the powerful extended families of the nobility, the government attempted to remake the city into a spatially unified whole. Straight, wide streets were the primary instruments of change. The new roadways rationalised the city's space and improved hygiene. More important, they established a system of public space protected by the new merchant regime that tied all the areas of the city together. Roadways replaced the courts at the centre of private precincts as the focus of architectural design. The street system converged on the centre of town, where the great buildings that served the whole community were prominently sited.

This architectural vision has had a lasting effect on all Western urban design. The great cities of modern Europe have monumental cores and comprehensive systems of public thoroughfares. Squares and streets provide the sites for building; architecture looks outward with elaborate facades. The late Middle Ages pioneered this urban structure but even in Florence the rebuilding of the environment was never completed. A long history of habitation marked the city in ways that had little to do with the new values. Even the ambitious government of the priors could not completely transform a city whose origins reached back to antiquity. To appreciate the most comprehensive schemes of the merchant commune we must look to the new towns. At San Giovanni and the other towns, Florentine planners not only represented the capital city, they perfected it. These were the ideal cities of the merchant commune. Thus, a study of the new towns is a study of Florence itself.

Plans

The plans of Florentine new towns form a distinctive family of orthogonal designs. They share essential qualities, despite diverse physical circumstances and the evolution of new-town planning during the 14th century. All the plans address a common set of problems and conform to the same planning principles. The new towns had as their first task the collection of a loyal population and the creation of a strong defensive position. They were all connected to Florence by a road, granted market privileges, and assigned an administrative role in the new Florentine territorial state. The balance between these functions varied from town to town. At Scarperia and Firenzuola the military situation was unusually perilous; Terranuova's character was heavily influenced by the fragmentation of its population; San Giovanni was the capital of the vicarate of the entire upper Valdarno; and Castelfranco was the centre only for the league of villages in its immediate vicinity. These circumstances had a significant influence on the way the towns developed. Today each settlement has its own distinct character; at the

moment of foundation, however, the plans were much less varied.

Assigned the task of selecting a site, Florentine town builders consistently chose flat ground. Hilltop locations and steep slopes were used for fortified retreats, but never for the new towns. Whether on the valley floor or on an upland plateau, only the most regular terrain would do. If nature had imperfections, Florentine officers ordered earth-moving operations to correct them. On the resulting standardised ground, the new towns conformed to a single basic pattern with two variations, both of which appear in the foundations of 1299. San Giovanni's plan, with its extended central square, was reused at Scarperia and Firenzuola. The plan of Castelfranco, whose distinctive feature is a square with proportions of 9:7, served as the inspiration for the plans of Terranuova and Giglio Fiorentino.

Orthogonality is the basis of Florentine new-town design, as it is for all of the most ambitious planning schemes of the Middle Ages. 14th-century city dwellers considered straight streets beautiful and a public ornament; town planners combined them in parallel and perpendicular relationships, however, for practical reasons. In the Middle Ages it was only on an orthogonally articulated plane that the precise location of a point could be known. Orthogonality facilitated the co-ordination of the parts of a composition and simplified the calculation of area. Only in the Renaissance did surveyors develop the techniques that allowed them to construct mathematically accurate maps of irregular geographic and urban forms. Before that time the space of the natural world was measured approximately. In the late Middle Ages, comprehensive urban design was possible only with the aid of the simple and consistent rules of orthogonality.

The description of Giglio Fiorentino illustrates that size was the town planners' first concern. There were many practical reasons why it was important. The amount of land to be acquired, and therefore the total cost, depended on the project's size, as did the number of immigrants the new settlement could accommodate. In providing dimensions, the planners also fixed the line of the town's defenses. This had a fundamental effect on the town's design. The ditches and palisades that the founders built and that succeeding generations reinforced with stone structures were essential to the open character of the plan. Without this defensive outline the continuous street system and the generous central square, features that were so important to a new-town plan, would have been impossible. The houses of the first settlers would have been huddled together for protection, and this first cell would surely have left its mark on the fully developed street system. The houses themselves might have formed the defensive barrier, as do the thick, windowless rear walls of a circle of houses in many Tuscan villages.

Over the centuries the population of Florentine new towns grew, but future immigration was not a primary consideration of the city's settlement scheme. The towns were intended for a particular group of settlers, and the plans showed no provisions for physical growth. The wall that defended a new community also confined it. Any expansion beyond the defenses had little in common with the layout of the original plan. At first, suburbs grew along the roads from the town gates. In the 19th and 20th centuries the pattern of expansion has responded to the requirements of garden villas and tall apartment blocks. San Giovanni and Scarperia, the most flourishing of the new towns today, offer the best examples.

Finite size and fixed shape were uncommon in medieval new towns. The 12th-century town of Bern, which expanded in three smoothly seamed stages along the axis of the town's broad market street, was characteristic of the flexibility of most medieval plans. Towns founded after 1255 by the administration of Alphonse de Poitiers in the county of Toulouse were laid out according to an open-ended survey system. Sainte-Foy-la-Grande on the Dordogne river and Montreal in the present-day department of Gers, both dating from the first year of Alphonse's town building campaign, are good examples of this town type. The formal theme of these plans is based on two pairs of parallel streets oriented at right angles to one another. The square space enclosed by their intersection was the market, where inauguration ceremonies, including the raising of a staff with the founder's coat of arms, took place. In the years immediately following the foundation of towns of this kind sometimes only the sides of the square were inhabited but as the town grew the four streets structured further development. Along one axis, the distance between the two streets – the width of the market – established the amount of space between all the parallel streets. Along the other axis a larger interval dictated the size of the rectangular blocks that most efficiently accommodated the town's row houses. This system could be infinitely enlarged. In both Sainte-Foy and Montreal the streets and blocks multiplied in good order, but expansion has now pushed the market place, still the functional centre of the community, to one side of the inhabited area.

Such asymmetry had no place in the Florentine concept of new-town design. Unforeseen circumstances could force the city's officials to approve construction that unbalanced a new-town plan, as was the case in Scarperia, but no town was designed as anything other than an essentially symmetrical composition. The principal axis of symmetry of every plan was a section of the main road that ran through the site. As the town's main street, the road determined the orientation of the blocks and of the majority of the town's remaining streets and alleys. The description of Giglio Fiorentino conveys the importance of the idea of symmetry around the main street. The description lists Giglio's streets, and the lots abutting them, in an orderly way, beginning at the town's edge and working toward the main street. It then gives the depth of the lots on the main street and the width of the main street itself, and concludes by saying that 'in the other part of the town, houses and streets shall be made as designated above,' ie, symmetrically.

As the axis of symmetry, the *via maestra* received special treatment and influenced the plan of a new town in a number of ways. It was the widest in the town and, as at Giglio, the houses along its sides had to observe special architectural requirements. Its orientation was the orientation of the town. All the Florentine plans were rectangular: the early designs (San Giovanni and Scarperia) had proportions of about 22:1, the later ones (Firenzuola, Terranuova, Giglio) slightly less than 2:1. Even Castelfranco, which was almost square, had one axis longer than the other. There, too, the axis of the main street dominated.

Midway along the main street of a new town and at the middle of the area enclosed by its defensive perimeter, there was a public piazza. In some of the towns this space was approximately square, in some it was rectangular, but in every case it was the focus of the plan and the centre of public life. The position of the square was fixed by a cross axis that stretched between the gates in the middle of the town's long walls. The cross axis sometimes took the form of a street, sometimes the square itself extended almost the entire distance between the walls. In either case this axis generated a secondary symmetry. Few streets and no blocks of house lots were oriented with the cross axis, but the arrangement of elements on one side of it mirrored the arrangement on the other, echoing the rigorous symmetry around the axis of the town's main street.

The two axes that fixed the position of the square also divided the towns into four quarters. These quarters were the residential areas and were densely packed with houses on lots from 10 to 12 *braccia* (5.84 to 7 metres) wide and 10 to 38 *braccia* (5.84 to 22.2

metres) deep. The centre of each quarter, except in the Giglio Fiorentino plan, was marked by a secondary intersection, and the streets that defined these crossings combined to make a circle around the centre of town. The wall of the town reflected the same idea, wrapping itself tightly around the settlement.

All the elements of a new-town plan were closely integrated in the Florentine designs. Conceived as finite objects, the towns were laid out symmetrically and with a powerful central element. These are designs that are subject to the same formal laws as single buildings and this, in the context of medieval urban design practice, is their most distinctive characteristic.

The pre-eminent form-giving element of a Florentine new town was the section of intercity road that ran between the two main gates. This road brought life to the community and its importance is reflected in its generous width and its central position. The property that bordered the main street was the most valuable in the town, being immediately in the path of arriving travellers. The town statutes reinforced this advantage by limiting the ability of merchants and hostellers to advertise their services. In a regulation that began, 'That no one may enrich himself at the cost of others, but rather be content with that which naturally comes his way', the hostellers, wine sellers, and merchants of Scarperia were prohibited from approaching any passer-by to solicit trade. Even when the conversation was initiated by the prospective customer, the vendor could not step more than 2 *braccia* (1.17 metres) from the door of his place of business to respond. Specifically prohibited was the practice of sending scouts to solicit customers on the main street or at the town's gates. All of this was particularly disadvantageous to those who did not have their establishments in plain view of the traveller.

It is understandable, then, that one of the goals of the Florentine planners was to give frontage on the main street to as many of the settlers as possible. Contemporary housing practice suggested the way to do this. The base unit of new-town design was the row house. The lots that accommodated these modest structures were rectangular, with their short sides fronting onto the street. Frontage was determined by the width of a single room. Larger houses attained their greater space by increased depth and additional stories, not, in the 14th century at least, by extended frontage. Neighbouring structures abutted one another, combining to form long blocks that were interrupted only infrequently by cross streets.

While neither the row house nor the extended block was an innovation of new-town planners, the close co-ordination of the rows of lots and the street plan had not been frequently applied elsewhere. In Florence, especially in the areas closest to the last circle of walls, the streets were so far apart that the buildings lining them consumed a very small part of the available ground. The remaining area functioned as garden and farmland or, occasionally, as a work area, until new streets were developed to open up this internal frontier. In the new towns these hidden spaces were eliminated. The streets were only as far from one another as the depth of the house lots between them.

The only large, open space in a Florentine new town was the piazza located at the intersection of the two axes of the plan, at the centre of the area enclosed by the circuit of the town walls. The *palazzo* of the Florentine official, the town hall, the town's main church, the oratories of the oldest confraternities, and the town's first convents were placed around, and in one case within, this central square. On its open ground religious festivals and public ceremonies were celebrated. The Florentine official took his oath of office in the square, and the population assembled to hear a reading of the town's statutes there. At Firenzuola town residents made public announcements in the square to clear real estate titles, and were obliged to gather there to celebrate the

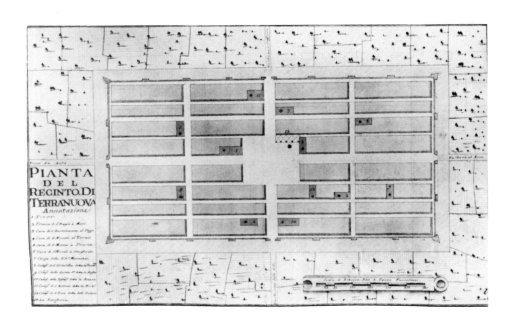

TERRANUOVA, PLAN, 1779

feast day of Florence's patron saint.

The central squares of the new towns as they now survive are strongly marked by these solemn uses. Their large scale and the public buildings that surround them give the squares a ceremonial character that seems appropriate to the formalities of church and state. The mundane functions of town life, however, also took place on this open ground. The most regular and significant of these activities was the market.

Almost all the new towns founded in Europe since the 9th century used their central square as a market place. This can be seen in the bastides of south-western France, in the German colonial towns in eastern Europe, and in the settlements in Swabia, Bavaria, and Austria, which represent the most numerous, the most carefully planned, and the most influential newtown schemes of the later Middle Ages. The Florentine conception of the square as the centre of ceremony is unusual. If it was not part of the original Florentine new-town idea, the city's planners did commit themselves to it before the end of their activity as founders of towns. The evidence from Firenzuola and Scarperia shows they thought of the central square in this way by the early decades of the 15th century. The foundation document for Giglio Fiorentino pushes the date of their acceptance of the idea back to the middle of the 14th century. At the same time as the Florentines were expanding the space dedicated to public assembly in front of their own town hall, the Palazzo dei Signori, their new-town planners explicitly placed the market in the last of the city's foundations 'outside of the town'. The square at Giglio was reserved for the palace of the Florentine official, the loggia for ceremonial events connected with it, and the church of the new parish. This design marks a turning point in the Florentine attitude toward the central squares of the new towns. From 1350 forward the squares are increasingly treated as

monumental spaces. The market was moved outside of the town to make way for buildings of a new scale and quality and functions associated with the administration and representation of the Florentine state.

The regularity of the piazza was only the most prominent evidence of the formal rigour that set the Florentine new towns apart from all other contemporary urban plans. The fixed overall dimensions, the double symmetry generated by the two perpendicular axes, the non-serial nature of the blocks and streets, the perfect centrality of the main square site, the repetition of the motif of intersection at critical points throughout the plan, and the synchronisation of the systems of circulation and defense were all equally rare qualities in the 14th century; their coordination in a single composition was a unique achievement. Fixed dimensions created an opportunity that the Florentine planners did not fail to exploit. The application of a system of diminishing block depths and the establishment of neighbourhood centres in the middle of each quarter were possible only in a town of finite size. The area within the walls was understood as a field of composition, like the surface inside the frame of an altar panel or the ground to be covered by a building. The arrangement of the streets, square, and building lots responded not just to the requirements of utility and regularity but also to those of formal design. In contrast to the open-ended systems of Bern and Sainte-Foy-la-Grande, the Florentine towns were complete at the moment of their foundation; they asked only to be filled with the families designated for relocation inside their walls.

Models

The tradition of the town foundation in western Europe stretches back to antiquity. From the 8th through the 5th century B C

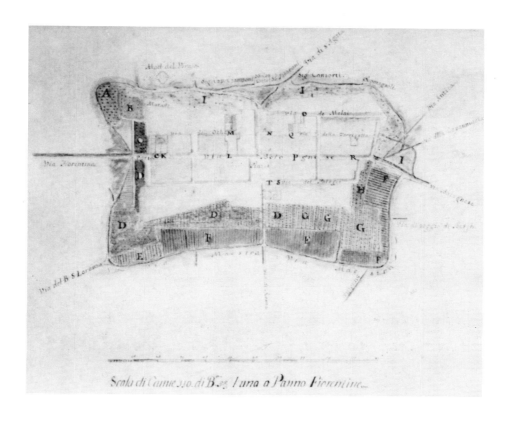

SCARPERIA, PLAN, AFTER 1776

Sicily and southern Italy were colonised by immigrants from the Greek homeland, who lived in founded towns at the centre of new city-states. Half a millenium later, Rome expanded its empire by creating territories inhabited and administered from newly made urban centres. Throughout the Middle Ages, in Great Britain and on the continent, notably in the south-west of France and in eastern Europe, conquest and development of land was accomplished by the *ex novo* creation of towns. Many of these settlements were laid out on orthogonal plans. Greek Agrigento, Roman Trier, and the 13th-century Sainte-Foy-la-Grande were all based on straight streets that intersected at right angles. Beyond this, however, the towns were very little alike. Their streets had different widths and were arranged in different patterns. Their blocks were sized and proportioned differently to suit different building types. Their public spaces took many shapes and related in different ways to the rest of the plan. Orthogonal planning has successfully accommodated the urban life of widely divergent civilisations precisely because it offers so many options.

As latecomers to the foundation of towns, the Florentines could look to earlier projects for instruction. There were precedents for the collection of populations, the establishment of markets and parishes, and the organisation of town and provincial governments, as there were for the design of town plans. Each plan element – squares, street systems, lot patterns – had been developed in many alternative forms. As their designs show, the Florentine town builders knew and used a wide range of this information.

The colonies of antiquity are sometimes cited as the ultimate source for medieval orthogonal designs. This interpretation seems especially compelling in the case of towns founded by a former Roman colony, as Florence itself was. In fact, the plans of most ancient urban sites survived to the 14th century in a confusing state of preservation. The changes that swept the Arno valley in the early Middle Ages, for example, had obliterated most of Florence's 1st-century plan. Literary sources contained a minimal amount of useful information about physical planning but they did succeed in firing the imagination of medieval planners. The foundation of Vittoria, the ill-fated town with which Frederick II hoped to replace the city of Parma, began at a moment selected by court astrologers with a ceremony in which the emperor traced the perimeter of the site with a plough in imitation of the ancient ritual of cutting the sulcus.

New-town planning had moved away from the model of the Roman colonies at least 400 years before the foundation of the Florentine towns. A dramatic illustration of this break is offered by the plan of Winchester, England. Originally the colony of Venta Belgarum, the site had lost its Roman street grid by the 5th century. Only the town wall and the street that ran between its east and west gates survived into the Middle Ages. Because of the site's defenses, Alfred the Great, King of Wessex, chose it for his new capital at the end of the 9th century. In the planning of the refounded town only the old main street maintained its position; nothing else of the Roman grid – based on blocks 135 metres square – was reconstructed. The medieval plan, preserved in the modern city, was made up of two kinds of rectangular blocks. The first lay on either side of the High Street and had its long axis parallel with the main road. Behind these blocks, and separated from them by a back street, were blocks that were arranged with their long axis perpendicular to the main street, extending uninterrupted to the town wall. Houses faced the streets that bordered these 80-metre-deep blocks on either side. The blocks on the main street, on the other hand, had a depth of only 31 metres and supported a single file of houses facing onto

87

the High Street where the town market was held. The varied size and orientation of the blocks of medieval Winchester destroyed the homogeneity of the Classical plan. In its place there was a focus, in this case on a main street, which was primarily functional but also formal, and was characteristic, in one way or another, of most of the new-town designs for the next one thousand years.

It is from these origins that medieval new-town planning developed, and by the end of the 13th century many hundreds of towns had been planned and planted. The men in charge of the San Giovanni and Castelfranco projects were far more likely to have looked to these contemporary designs than to the remnants of the thirteen-hundred-year-old plan of Florence's city centre. To do so they would not have had to search far beyond the borders of Florentine territory. The city's ally in the Arno valley, the Guelph city of Lucca, was engaged in the same effort to expand her territorial holdings as was Florence. In the middle of the 13th century Lucca turned to a new-town strategy. Her towns, like the Florentine towns that followed them, began as resettlement sites for the serfs of the city's baronial rivals and grew into capitals of the Lucchese territorial state. They, too, were on important roads, served military functions, and became the economic centres of the surrounding countryside.

Planners

Orthogonal street systems testify to the careful planning that preceded the settlement of hundreds of medieval new-town sites. In very few cases, however, can one point with any certainty to the identity or even the professional character of the men who prepared the designs. The more important the surviving documents, the less they tell about the design. In the most ceremonial papers – the acts of foundation and the charters of liberties to the settlers – the physical details of the new towns, when mentioned at all, are presented as decisions of the founder himself. The tradition of the lord's personal responsibility for his works was a venerable one, and was evident in the first new-town document of the post-antique period. In this charter, dated 1120, for the foundation of Freiburg im Breisgau, it is the Zähringer duke Conrad himself who, in the language of the document, 'set in place' the market town and 'distributed' the building lots.

Even when a prince delegated the authority for a foundation, the persons named in the documents are administrative, not technical, assistants. The three men Edward I of England appointed in 1283 'to plan and assess the new town of Yharnme [New Winchelsea] . . . to plan and give directions for streets and lanes necessary for two churches . . . to assign and to deliver to the barons competent places according to the requirements of their state, and to provide and give directions concerning harbours and all other things necessary for the town' were Stephen de Pencestre, Gregory de Rokesle, and Henry le Waleys, government officials and businessmen. The French royal foundations offer the example of the notary Pons Maynard who in 1255 was empowered 'to establish the charter and the consuls of the town- and trace the streets, blocks, and lots and to assign them' at Montreal in the Agenais.

Whether French or English, the ceremonial documents identify only men with legal responsibility for the planning of new towns. If the project enjoyed the specialised services of a surveyor or a professional drawn from the building trades, such an assistant was not listed in the official record. The evidence from Florence is quite different. The archives of the town-founding committees that were appointed to act for the government go beyond legislative documentation to preserve contracts and accounts of expenses. Part of the information contained in this daily record is the identity of the new-town planners.

The administration by Florence of new-town projects evolved as the city gained experience. The records for the first towns are of the usual, formal sort; where they reveal anything about the organisation of the projects, they are tentative, and give the impression that the system for building towns was experimental . . .The character of the Florentine records changed in the second quarter of the 14th century with the formation of autonomous committees devoted to town building . . . In the mid-14th century Florentine town building – although not specifically the foundation of towns – was at its peak. Administration of the many projects was almost exclusively in the hands of individually constituted committees, each of which was responsible for one or at most two projects.

The men who served on the new-town committees had no professional training as builders, surveyors, or designers. Their only qualification was to be part of the section of the Florentine population that participated in city government. Their activity on the town building committees was a civic obligation like many others they fulfilled. Their work required only occasional meetings and their obligation was usually only for six months. The four-member Vicchio committee of 1365, for example, included men who belonged to the Calimala, the Lana, and the Cambio guilds of the city's merchant community. One of them, Nofrio Johanis domine Lapi Amolfi, served a second term, but that was the limit of his involvement in town foundation work.

The inexperience of the Florentine committee men and the sophistication of the town plans they dealt with presents a paradox that we can understand only by recognising the limits of the committee men's responsibility. It was the duty of the citizens who served on the town building agencies to define and to protect Florentine interests in all aspects of the projects. They cannot, however, have been expected either to initiate all the ideas that went into the creation of the towns or to execute their decisions. The great contribution of the documents preserved in the archives of the Ufficiali delle Castella is that they reveal how the agencies worked and what kind of assistants they employed. From them we learn about the longevity of the salaried staff: in the face of the regular rotation of non-specialised committee men, it was the staff that lent experience and continuity to the administration of the projects.

The admirable town plans of San Giovanni, Castelfranco, and Terranuova are the result of a co-operative effort between two types of contributors: members of government named in the official acts of foundation and professional designers recorded in the documents of the town building committees. The heart if the Florentine political establishment actively participated in planning the new-town projects. Head of the government oversaw the first projects; respected members of the guild regime manned the committees that took over this custodianship on the 1330s. The committees were involved in many issues of state embodied in Florentine new-town policy: they selected sites and settlers; decided on markets, roads, tax freedoms, and defensive goals. They did not, however, presume to do the technical work of laying out the town any more than they would have built the town walls. For these specialised tasks professional designers were employed, introducing a level of formal sophistication that the town plans would not otherwise have had.

---------- * ----------